JUST TRY

ONE MORE

PENNY LEE DEAN

BALBOA
PRESS

A DIVISION OF HAY HOUSE

Balboa Press books may be ordered through booksellers or by contacting:

Balboa Press
A Division of Hay House
1663 Liberty Drive
Bloomington, IN 47403
www.balboapress.com
1 (877) 407-4847

Printed in the United States of America.

ISBN: 978-1-4525-8499-7 (sc)
ISBN: 978-1-4525-8500-0 (e)

Balboa Press rev. date: 12/30/2013

DEDICATION

I am dedicating this book to my mother, my family, and my ocean teammates. I am also dedicating this book to Siga who taught me to believe in myself and become a stronger swimmer and a better coach. I thank her for all she did for me. Lastly, I would like to thank all of my coaches from Spud Abbot, Charlie Sava, Ray and Zada Taft, George Haines and Claudia Kolb, Nort Thorton, Jim Montrella, Tennie Barnes, and Gary Troyer.

I wrote this book to inspire others to *Just Try One More*. I hope each of you conquer your goals!

LIST OF PHOTOGRAPHS

Cover—Penny warming up feet in English Channel

Penny preparing for mental swimming

Miss California, 1957

1st year Russian river, 1962

Dean Children-Penny 7, Barry 3, Brian 12, Carolyn 14

25,000 yard swim to raise money for English Channel swim

Party at Dottie York's home celebrating the various swim

Night of single crossing, leaving from Siga's

Getting ready for single crossing Wed 1st, 1976

Siga and Penny on skiff for double crossing

Siga greasing Penny as Boy Scouts cheering for the swimmer

Start of swim of double of the swim

Mrs. Cleveland gave me a dozen red roses

Dinard, France Training Beach—tide is out

Beginning of the 36,000 meter swim

Part way through the 36,000 meter swim

Finish with 3 pacers—World Record by 20 minutes

Training spot, low tide in Folkestone, England

Harbor in Folkestone, England low tide

Penny entering water on choppy day

Outdoor sea pool, unheated

White Cliffs of Dover, Shakespeare Beach start of swim

Grease up on way to Shakespeare beach

Completed greasing up

In dingy on way to beach

Townsend Passenger Liner passing at 45 minutes

Frances taking stroke counts

Penny feeding, Barry holding pole

Penny swimming through kelp

Sealink from France, France in background

Wind picking up

Wind getting rougher and started to rain
One mile to go
Penny walking on shore
Penny walking to skiff
Penny and Mom hugging on skiff
Penny temperature taken by Dr. Smith
Temperature taken a long minute
Penny warming up in sleeping bag
Penny at party after swim
Ray and Audrey Scott at party
Nancy Smith, Penny, and Dr. Smith
Six days after English Channel swim 17 mile Winderamere
First women at Chicago, 3 weeks after England—10 mile swim
1982 World Cup Team—Dean, Patterson, Munatones
Assistant Coaches for English Channel Relay
1990 English Channel World Record—single and double
1991 Perth World Championship Team
1991 Pan Pacific Championship Team
1991 Pan Pacific Coaches
Penny and Katrina resting
Frances, Katrina and Penny at Disneyland
Penny and Katrina at Haldemen Pool preparing for Halloween
Katrina and Penny in crib
Our family—Claudia, Penny and Katrina in Alaska 2009
1979 Receiving Rolex watch for fastest swim of summer

Contents

Introduction xi

My Family Relationships 1

A Step Up? 11

Pomona College And A New Career 16

Ocean Circuit, 1975 23

Third Season At Pomona College 31

Preparation For The Catalina Swim 35

One Month To Go 39

Catalina Here I Come 48

The After Affects 59

The Final Year At Pomona College 66

To Begin Again 71

The Tests 78

The Double Crossing 87

The Watson Fellowship 113

The Final Leg 126

The Finishing Touches 137

Is That The Coast? 142

Epilogue 167

INTRODUCTION

My hands were sweating profusely as I tightened my grip on the rubber handles of the crutches. The cold wet sand tingled between my toes. Seventy other swimmers stood beside me, awaiting the start of the Santa Cruz one mile pier swim. It had been just a month since I lay in a hospital bed preparing for a knee operation. I still had not walked without crutches. For three days I had been able to swim, for therapy, the doctor said, but nothing strenuous. For five months, the longest layoff of my swimming career, I had been out of the water. At nineteen, I was considered over the hill. Should I quit swimming after this year? What was left for me? How could I make a comeback at nineteen? Would I fade out as so many other swimmers had at college? Or would I continue?

I knew I had to continue. I had not completed my dream: to swim the English Channel. Until I did, I could not quit swimming.

This dream emerged when I was ten years old. By my tenth birthday I had been swimming for over eight years, first on a country-club level in San Mateo, California, then on an AAU team in San Francisco coached by Olympic coach Charlie Sava.

After three years, the daily commuting (about one and a half hours, depending on traffic) had taken its toll on me and my family. It was too difficult for my family so, therefore, I began training with Ray and Zada Taft of the San Mateo Marlins. This is where my dream of swimming the English Channel emerged.

One day, Ray came to me and asked if I wanted to swim the length of the Golden Gate Bridge. I was ten years old at the time. If I completed the swim, I would be the youngest female to have done so. However, this was not the purpose of the swim. The point was that regardless of a person's age she could learn to swim and that drowning was pointless. Another teammate, eight-year old Bruce Farley, would also make an attempt.

Bruce was about fifty-two inches tall and weighed about eighty pounds. I, on the other hand, was fifty inches tall and weighed a mere fifty pounds.

One afternoon we had the distinct honor to speak with Gertrude Ederle. She was the first woman to swim the English Channel, and did so in record time in 1926. She told us not to swim in cold water as we would go deaf, but if we wanted to do it, then good luck! If we began prior to the tide change, the swim was only a mile in distance and would take about twenty-five minutes. If the tide changed, instead of a calm swim, we would encounter water rushing back out to sea. This gradually picks up speed until it reaches a maximum of nine miles per hour. Another difficulty was the water temperature. The swim was planned for mid-September. During this month, the water temperature ranges from the high fifties to the low sixties—not the best temperatures for swimming.

In order to become acclimatized to the cold water, the Tafts had us train in the San Francisco Bay once or twice, and in the 100 yard Fleishacher's Salt Water Pool in San Francisco. After successfully completing the various stages of training, it was decided that we would swim on Saturday, September 18, 1965.

What a day! I can vividly remember it. The air was filled with excitement and a sense of apprehension.

Various newspaper reporters wanted interviews, and someone asked me to stand at the edge of the pier and gaze towards the bridge—the Golden Gate. It looked like a gigantic orange metallic monster with outstretched arms grasping the land for support, and at the same time it was beautiful.

Later, Bruce and I watched an old fisherman as he struggled to pull in his line. His face strained with pain as he lifted the fish onto the dock. It was a shark. I had never been so close to a shark before. It was only a baby, maybe two feet in length, but it seemed as big as me. A reporter had us stand by the shark for pictures. I said with a smile, "He probably couldn't bite off more than a finger or a toe."

Our coaches quickly ushered us from that end of the pier. Everyone was getting a little anxious because the eight o'clock starting time had come and gone. The swim had been delayed because the motor of the support vessel would not start. Almost an hour had passed by the time Bruce and I climbed into the boat to leave for the starting point off the rocks at Fort Point. We would be swimming from the San Francisco side to the Marin side. The delay created some problems that could not be overcome. The tide was changing under the bridge and at the later time there was more of a possibility of encountering merchant ships.

As the boat approached the rocks, it was decided that no grease would be applied to our bodies. The swim could not be delayed further. However, the water temperature was in the high fifties.

Quickly we entered the water to begin our ever-changing swim. The expected one-half hour swim was extended due to the vicious tides we encountered under the bridge. As we slowly approached the halfway point, we were abruptly stopped. A huge sugar ship was approaching. We were instructed to tread water until the ship had passed. If we had been too close, we would have been sucked under the ship. For fifteen minutes we floated motionless. I was very cold. All the while I kept thinking that maybe we should have applied the grease to our bodies so that we may have been warmer.

Finally, we started swimming, only to be stopped less than fifteen minutes later. Again we had to tread water. I was miserable. I do not remember complaining, but within ten minutes after starting up again, Zada asked me if I wanted to get out.

She asked me! I was cold and tired, so I gave up. I quit. As I climbed up onto the boat and watched Bruce complete the last four hundred yards, I cried.

After Bruce finished, the boat rushed back to the dock. Everyone was very happy for him. As I climbed up the stairs to the dock, I looked for my mother. She had walked away. I had failed.

Looking at the Golden Gate Bridge, I promised myself right then that I would never quit again, no matter what. Someday I would swim the English Channel and break the world record.

My Family Relationships

The story of my swimming is inextricably entwined with the story of my relationship with my mother. When she walked away from me at the Golden Gate swim; I was crushed. Afterwards, she did not say anything to me about the swim, or asked what had happened. I was ten years old, and had to figure out for myself what was wrong.

My mother started my swimming career when I was only one year old, but she did so indirectly. When my older sister was seven, she spent nearly all her free time reading. My mother decided she needed physical activity, so my older brother and sister were enrolled in swim lessons at the Elks Club in San Mateo. Although only a year old at the time, the coach, Spud Abbott, put me in swimming lessons. Immediately, I started swimming. Spud ran carnivals all around the Bay area to promote his club and swimming, so, at less than two years old, he made me part of the entertainment because I could swim across the pool. I could even jump off the diving board and swim the length of the pool.

Miss California, 2 years old

During that time, I wore a two-piece gold bikini and a huge white cap. Although not yet a very good walker, I could swim! I did this until I was five, and then joined the Elks Club team. As it turned out, swimming individually was fine, but when I was on a relay, I ran for the bathrooms to hide.

Penny, age 7, at Russian River

By the time I was seven, our family had changed clubs to the San Francisco Recreation & Park Swim Club (SFRP) in San Francisco, coached by Charlie Sava. I was already doing double workouts. My father would drive me up to practice early in the morning for an hour and a half workout. After which I would walk the two blocks to the trolley car, take the trolley car to the bus station and take a bus to San Mateo. I would walk the two blocks to school at Saint Mathews Episcopal Day School. After school I would walk three blocks to the train station and ride it to San Francisco. I would leave the station, cross the street, go to a newspaper stand and sit on a pile of newspapers and wait for my dad to pick me up. My dad would pick me up from his work as a lawyer for an insurance company and take me to swimming practice.

I always tried to ride the train without paying the eighty-five cents for the ticket so that I would have money for candy. Those days I ate too much and would throw up at practice. Needless to say, the first time I threw up and my mom found out, I had to stop not paying and thus eating candy. I would swim for two hours then we would drive the twenty-five minutes back to San Mateo.

During this time, we attended, as a team, the Russian River swims. Legally, you couldn't swim the women's mile until you were twelve, but starting when I was seven, my father and I would walk up stream to the starting cement plank. I would swim out to the plank, and climb up and wait for the boats to arrive filled with the "legal" twelve and older swimmers. For five years we did this, with me finishing in the top four each year—unofficially.

Dean children

After three years at SFRP, we moved to the Millbrae Otters for one season. My sister, Carolyn, and my older brother, Brian, drove me during this time. Brian set a speed record for the drive to Millbrae, and one for how many times he could change lanes on El Camino Real on the way to Millbrae. The next year my younger brother, Barry, and I tried out for the Santa Clara Swim Club. We were accepted. Unfortunately, this move would bring out my mother's true nature.

My mother had two sides to her. She could be supportive and enthusiastic; and then she was anxious, angry, and acted like nothing was good enough. She became obsessed with my career; so obsessed, that she moved us periodically to different teams, especially after my older brother and sister quit swimming. Many of the team changes were the right moves. She recognized my talent and was totally invested in making sure I had a chance to make the Olympic swim team. She was prone to loud and irrational rants, especially during swim practice, but I loved to swim, so rarely did they get to me. Although I was embarrassed when they happened in front of other people, I didn't stand up to her. I just swam harder, trying to please her and myself.

When I was twelve, our family split into two parts. Barry and I went to live in Santa Clara with my mother while Carolyn and Brian stayed in San Mateo with my dad. My father worked in San Francisco. Even though we were only an hour's drive away, he would come down to visit us only on the weekends. If we didn't have a meet, we would go to San Mateo. However, my dad would almost always fight with my mom on Friday, and then leave on Saturday. It became a pattern with him.

After one meet in which I swam poorly and didn't make the finals, my mother and I returned to our apartment. Once home, my mother tried to commit suicide. She said it was a sunny day and the rest of our family wasn't around. She made me promise not to call the police or any other emergency service. She also said she had found me a family to live with so I could keep swimming, and gave me a bank book. She didn't say she was sorry.

Once I realized that she was incoherent, I snuck downstairs and called my dad. My brother answered the phone. He sounded very irritated. Everyone there was having a nice day together. He was mad because I had interrupted his day! I asked to speak to Dad. I spoke to my dad about Mom and told him to call the police and tell them to break open the door because my mother had made me lock all the locks on the door. Within five minutes the police arrived, broke in the door and dealt with my mother. I had to ride in the police car and explain what had happened. I said that I thought that she had tried to commit suicide because I hadn't swum fast enough and she was pissed off. Years later I found out that my father had served her with divorce papers that week. (She had not told us.) After this, she spent three months in a mental institution. She saved her pills and tried again, because my dad had her served a second time while she was in the hospital. Her psychiatrist at the hospital had recommended he do so this at that time so she would be where she could get immediate help. When we arrived that night to visit her and were told what had happened, I leaped over the counter to grab the nurse. I was angry that my mother was able to acquire pills and attempt another suicide under their watch! Being only four foot nine, my father caught me mid-air and pulled me back.

Once home, my mother took pills all the time and attempted suicide on a regular basis. She did not ever take enough to kill herself, just enough to have me stay home on weekends or have to leave sleepovers early to check on her and then watch her. It was a tough few years with my mother, but with the right care, she finally recovered. Thankfully, a drug company invented Prozac!

My dad stayed away as much as possible during this time. Eventually, we learned that he was having an affair with a woman whom he later married. Also, he was an alcoholic and had a violent temper. He would come home from work late, work in the garage, where he was really drinking, then go to bed. With such limited time with him, I really didn't get to know him until I was in my twenties. The last year of his life I visited him regularly and talked with him daily. During our visits, we shared our love for football together. This time with him helped me to know my father at last.

During this time, a normal day in our house began with breakfast then off to morning swim practice at 6:00 a.m. After an hour and a half of swimming, I went directly to school. When school was over, I was off to my second swim practice. The hard part of the day came next—dinner time. At dinner my mother would not eat with us. She ate in her bedroom. If we made too much noise, she would yell at us to be quiet. If we still weren't quiet enough, she would come in, act crazy and start screaming. Sometimes, after she left, we couldn't help but giggle. Most of the time, to us four kids, the rants made no sense. My father would whisper to us to be quiet, but it was usually to no avail. Ultimately, she would scream at us that dinner was over and told us to clear our plates.

My mother also became upset when we traveled for a long time. According to Carolyn, "When we had long drives for swimming meets, Mom would take a diuretic just before we left, and we would have to stop every twenty minutes for the whole trip." My father always built in this time, but he would still get angry. I was too young to know what my mother was doing or why, but later I learned that her hands and feet used to swell enormously and the diuretic helped lessen the swelling.

At one swim meet across the Bay when I had just missed qualifying for the Senior Nationals in the 500 freestyle, my mother came into the locker room. While I was dressing, she started yelling at me. The mother of one of my teammate's stepped in and told her to stop it and to back off. Assuming the woman was just some meddler, my mother swore at her, and then stormed out of the locker room. The rest of the meet we could not find my mother, and when the meet was over, she was nowhere in sight. We cruised the area for four hours, but did not find her. We returned to the meet to find her sitting under a tree. As usual, Barry and I were upset and worried, but my mother had only wanted to fight. She made me feel guilty because another parent had reached out to support me. It occurred to me then that in the future I would have to dress quickly so that she would not have time to abuse me verbally in public again. So, I learned to deck change. Deck changing is a streamlined way of getting dressed. First, you put on a t-shirt, then untie and pull down the top of your suit. Next, you wrap a towel around your bottom half, slide off your suit, and then slide on underwear and team sweat pants.

My parents fought, then, and soon afterwards we packed and finally left for home. It was a long ten-hour meet. We had been there four extra hours. My mother never apologized, explained herself or tried to make us feel better. Worse, on the freeway, half way home with my father driving sixty-five miles an hour, she tried to jump from the car. I caught her, as it was a feeble attempt, but I had had it. I was thirteen and decided that from then on whenever possible I would go to meets with friends.

Looking back, I realize my mother was overinvested in my swimming. She wanted me to make the Olympics, but I don't know why. It wasn't important to me, only swimming the English Channel.

My sister was the reader, my older brother the alcoholic, and I was the swimmer. My younger brother was the wild one. My sister also helped take care of Barry and me. Many times at school she pretended to be sick so she could come home and make sure that we were okay.

From the time I was twelve I had to take care of my mother. There were no boundaries in our relationship. She became my child, especially after every suicide attempt or fight with my father, and then after he moved out. Barry became so disgusted with her, he would leave home, unable to deal with her behavior.

During one of my parents' fights I stepped in between them and my hand was cut by a knife. My mother was holding the knife. Furious, my dad raced out and jumped into his car. My mother ran after him. While Barry and I held each other, we watched as my dad backed into my mother, knocking her down. Slowly, she pushed herself up, ran to her car, and chased after my father. I looked at my brother; his blue eyes were glazed over. He was crushed. That day he gave up on our family. He was eight years old and very mature.

I was lucky; I had my swimming. Along with school, it gave me stability with the two practices a day. Swimming kept me going and sane.

The one thing my mother did very well was plan a yearly vacation. On these, we went as far north as Canada and as far south as the border towns of Mexico. Mostly we camped, but the vacations were nice and usually had limited fighting. We would play cards, fish, talk, take long walks, and just enjoy ourselves. We ran into bears at Crater Lake, pirates at Disneyland and more. Also, Barry coin dipped for change in the Busch gardens in Seattle where he fell in the water. Our favorite trip was Yosemite. It offered so much to do and was so beautiful. Our least favorite was the trip Dad forgot the tent and we had to put up the canvas shelter he had brought instead, and, of course, it rained.

Birthdays and holidays were challenging. My mother planned exotic birthday parties which were fun. She also made sure each of us four kids received a present on one another's birthday, which made us feel special.

Holidays on the other hand were deadly, with Thanksgiving being the worst. My mother felt a major project such as cleaning out the refrigerator, painting the living room or cleaning the rugs should be done by anyone who was not helping with the cooking on Thanksgiving. One Thanksgiving during my freshman year of college the major project was for Barry and my dad to paint the living room. A half hour before dinner, my mother told them when dinner would be ready, but they weren't finished. They worked for forty minutes, and then started cleaning the brushes. Meanwhile, Mom and I had already finished cooking dinner and doing the dishes. She screamed, "If no one wants to eat, okay," and then took the turkey with the stuffing still in it and dumped it into the sink of dirty water. She then stormed to her room and locked the door. After cleaning up the mess, I called the airline and changed my ticket to return to school the next morning. I went to Mom's locked door and told her, but she didn't respond. From then on, Thanksgiving was another holiday I wouldn't go home for anymore.

Halloween and Easter were normally pretty good celebrations. In both cases, if one brother had more candy, it didn't matter as everything was dumped out and divided equally, well almost equally, as my mother always had a share.

Christmas was a nice holiday as long as we waited until my dad had finished putting all the presents together. Of course we didn't know this was why we had to wait. To us, it had to be Santa. After opening all our presents, we would have coffee cake and relax the rest of the day, then have a ham or turkey dinner.

Overall, my family was abusive, dangerous and crazy, and emotionally exhausting, with only occasional periods of peace. Swimming was the only thing that kept me sane and moving forward.

A Step Up?

By December of 1967, our home was now in Santa Clara, the home of the well known Santa Clara Swim Club, coached by George Haines. We, Mom, Barry, and I, settled in a small apartment a little over a mile from the pool, and started our new life together.

During the four years I swam with Santa Clara I did not develop as well as my mother and I had expected I would. George spent most of his time with the best swimmers, the Olympians, and not as much with other levels of swimmers, many of whom had lots of talent. However, I furthered my long distance career. Besides returning to the Healdsburg mile race and the two mile canal swim in Foster City, I began entering the AAU Long Distance Junior Nationals. This meet consisted of a senior three mile cable race for women, a four-mile cable race for men and other shorter races for various age groups. In 1968 and 1969 the Junior Nationals were held in Cull Canyon, a reservoir east of the San Francisco Bay.

In 1968 I entered the 13-14 year olds two-mile cable race, and was a member of the Santa Clara's seniors' team entry for the three-mile cable race. A team entry consisted of three swimmers. With me were Tracy Finneran and Joan McArthur, both nationally-ranked distance swimmers. I was not nationally-ranked yet. The team that scored the least points would win the trophy.

The course was four hundred and forty yards in length. A rope was stretched the length of the course and at each end were drum barrels as turnaround points. Every few hundred feet there were buoys to keep the rope on the surface for the three-mile race.

We were lined up diagonally for the start from the fastest to the slowest, with the latter near the beach. As the race began, Karen Moe (who would later win the 200 Fly in the Munich Olympics in 1972, and place fourth at the Montreal Olympics in 1976), then of the Aquabears, and Joan McArthur, took the lead, with Tracy and me battling for third and fourth respectively. It was a close race all the way. No one, except my mother, expected me to be so close to Tracy. As I rounded the buoy for the last time, I swung wide to the right. I was equal with Tracy, and I wanted to beat her. I pulled a few strokes in front of her. Everything was going well; there were only four hundred yards to the finish. For the finish we were supposed to touch an official boat. As I approached the finish, I lifted my head and saw that the boat was adjacent the barrel. I, on the other hand, was twenty yards off to the right side.

I had expected the boat to be in the center as announced. Tracy was only three feet behind me, but she was next to the rope. I had to swim diagonally towards the boat. Tracy touched me out by three tenths of a second. I was disappointed that I had lost, but I was very pleased with my swim. Many people were surprised at my ability to swim so quickly, for so far because I was not as talented in the pool as Tracy.

The next day I swam the two-mile cable race and won. George was very pleased with my performance, but I was dropped from his senior group. The rationalization was that I had not made the Senior Outdoor Nationals. As a result, I could not continue training with the National Unit. He could understand my success in longer distances, but not my inability to make Nationals in the 1500 meters. It was just too short for me.

In the next three years I moved from one group to another. I worked very hard, but always just missed qualifying for Senior Nationals.

As for my long distance swimming, I returned to the Junior Nationals in Cull Canyon in 1969. This time I was third, and Barbara Belagorsky and Star Fixott were first and second, respectively. Tracy, however, only swam the thirteen-fourteen year olds' two-mile on the second day. After swimming the three-mile the first day, I finished second to Tracy by three seconds in the two-mile the following day. My endurance abilities were becoming evident.

In 1970, the Junior Nationals for Long Distance Swimming were going to be held in the East while the Senior Long Distance Nationals were being held in the Mid-West. No one from Santa Clara had ever competed in the Senior Nationals. There had been no reason to, with the Junior Nationals being held in our own backyard. This year, however, George decided to take a team. I really wanted to go but I was not chosen. I was very disappointed.

In 1971, the Junior Nationals were held in Omaha, Nebraska. I asked if I could go since I knew I would not be chosen for the Senior Nationals. George said it was fine, but I had to pay my own way.

In Nebraska, I learned a lot. It was the first time I had someone drag off me in a race. Anne Watland, of the Omaha Westside Swim Club, rode on my feet, intending to pass me at the finish. She did a very good job. At the two-mile mark, I was so frustrated I could barely breathe. *Here I had come all this way, my mother spending all that money; I had to win!* I let Anne pass me so I could catch my breath and regain my confidence. I dragged off her for almost a fourth of a mile, but I wanted the lead back. I was not going to lose this one. As I circled the last buoy, I began to sprint, and left Anne in my wake. I won by a few seconds. I learned a lot from this race, not just strategy.

Prior to the swim, there had been a lot of newspaper coverage. I even told the press that I intended to break the record. However, on the day of the swim, it was very windy which made the swim very choppy and dispelled any chances of breaking the record. Conditions play a significant part in all long-distance races, whether they are in the ocean, a lake, or a river. This is the one reason why time commitments are very difficult to predict, and sometimes have disastrous results.

When I returned to Santa Clara, George told me that whenever I was on a trip representing Santa Clara, I was to name him as my coach. Since I hadn't been swimming in his group, I had listed Claudia Kolb, a friend I had worked with recently. He learned of this when my interview made the local television channel, and he was upset.

By the end of the summer, my mother decided that I would be leaving Santa Clara. I was very disappointed. My mother felt I needed a change because I was not doing as well in the pool as I was in the long distance swims.

This turned out to be a very good move for me. We joined the Foothill Aquatic Club, coached by Nort Thorton. Within the first year there I improved tremendously. I even qualified for the Senior Outdoor Nationals in three events.

My first Nationals were a learning experience. While there, I swam the 400 Free and the 400 IM, but I had to leave the meet two days early because the Healdsburg River race fell on the same weekend. I had won that race two years in a row, and if I won it three in a row, I would win the perpetual trophy. This would make me the second woman to do so, Star Fixott being the first, winning 1968-1970. Nort let me do it, but he was not too pleased. So I went, and thank goodness, I won.

At the end of the summer I went to the Munich Olympics with two of my teammates, Mike Johnson and Bill Chao, both outstanding swimmers with numerous records. We had been chosen by a committee representing the Robin Smith Memorial Fund. Robin Smith was a backstroker on the Foothill A.C. who was killed in a car accident. Instead of having people send flowers for the funeral, her parents asked people to donate money to this fund. Robin had wanted to go to the Olympics, so her parents felt this would be more appropriate. The trip was most inspirational. It lasted for a month in which we traveled to six countries, spending one full week at the Olympics.

During the years that I swam for Foothill, numerous other opportunities were also made available. For six months in 1973, Shane Gould, the Australian superstar, winner of five medals in Munich, trained with us.

At the 1973 Kentucky Outdoor Nationals I made an enormous drop in my time in the 1500 meter free. I had been seated forty-seventh, yet I finished twenty-third. It helped to have a coach who cared so much. Working with Nort was paying off.

Gradually, through an excellent weight program, he improved my strength. Furthermore, he taught me how to swim freestyle with a two-beat kick and how to negative split my swims. Negative split means to swim the second half of the race faster than the first half. Working with him, I also gained a better understanding of training myself, both physically and mentally, and of my capabilities. Nort taught me how to acknowledge pain, and then how to go beyond it. He believed that most swimming was mental, therefore, one had to learn about one's self, and what one wanted to achieve. He did a lot for my career.

POMONA COLLEGE AND
A NEW CAREER

A fter the completion of the 1973 season, I went to southern California to attend Pomona College in Claremont. It was not known as an athletic school, but for me now, education was the most important aspect of school, not swimming. Even so, the men's coach, Gary Troyer, seemed very enthusiastic and supportive. The college had also recently added a women's team, and Tennie Barnes was the coach.

As it turned out, going to Pomona College was the best decision of my life, not only from an educational standpoint, but for my long distance swimming career as well.

In my first season at Pomona, I swam with the men and the women, since the women's program was limited. The furthest event the women swam was the four-hundred yard freestyle. My best event, on the other hand, was the 1650 yard freestyle. This was why I wanted to swim for the men. I was only permitted to swim the 1000 and the 1650 for the men, events the women's program did not have.

The first year was very frustrating, though. As this extended season progressed, I encountered one disappointment after another. I did fairly well in the women's season, but I didn't make the end of the season drops I had expected. I easily qualified for Women's Nationals; however, since I swam for the men, I was told that I would not be able to attend the AIAW Nationals in the spring. This turned out to be incorrect. No one verified that I was qualified, and I didn't learn otherwise in time to compete.

My season with the men, which ran from December to March, went fairly well until I sprained my ankle three weeks before the championships. From then on, the season just seemed to fall apart. I did not make Nationals; my year was over.

Now what? I had never been free from training, but I did want a rest, though. At that time I began thinking about Sandra Keska, a top collegiate swimmer and nationally-ranked distance swimmer. She was training to swim the English Channel that summer. I had always wanted to swim it. If she could, why couldn't I? During the women's season, I had beaten her, and she had not beaten me in two years. Earlier, I had asked Tennie Barnes, the women's coach, if she would help me train for the English Channel. I had a lot of respect for her. Tennie was very supportive of what I was doing. Whenever I needed moral support she was very helpful. I felt I needed the moral support to make a successful crossing, so she agreed to help.

Once I began the intricate planning for the crossing, however, her initial enthusiasm waned. She did not want to be away for so long. Such a swim would involve three months of intensive training, and at least two weeks in England for the swim. This was my training philosophy for the Channel. Prior to the end of the semester, I planned to train in the ocean and, hopefully, at the local lake.

The biggest commitment would be money. To cover the training and the navigator's fee, I would need a few thousand dollars. In order to raise the money, I decided to have a swim marathon. The distance would be one thousand lengths in a twenty-five yard pool. That was twenty-five thousand yards. The swim was planned for 8:00 a.m., Sunday, June 9, 1974, the morning of graduation.

25,000 yard swim in a pool

The reasoning behind it was to attract the parents of the graduating seniors and their friends. In early May, explanation letters were sent to the parents and the students, and numerous hours were spent organizing this, but the responses were limited. Meanwhile, Tennie called Florence Chadwick. Not only had she swum the Channel in record time, many times, but she was Sandra Keska's trainer. Up to that time Tennie had not realized the intensity and time involved to successfully complete this endeavor. After her talk with Chadwick, she called the English, Channel Swimming Association to get further information.

Tennie's interest was fading quickly. She said if I trained myself, she would be willing to take me to England for the swim. Two weeks earlier, she had been eager, willing, but now realizing the totality of the project, she did not want to spend her whole summer training me. I did not want a part-time coach, however. Maybe I was asking a lot, maybe even too much, but I needed a full-time coach. As it was, I was having problems training myself in the mornings and afternoons. After having to do that all season, I could not see doing it all summer, too. I knew I would have to go off on my own, but also, I would have to find someone who was totally committed to my goal and to me.

Then, amidst all of the planning, in the third week of April 1974, I hurt my knee after a women's water polo game. Why now? I was just getting enthusiastic about the Channel. So, I went to a knee specialist who gave me a shot of Cortisone, and told me to use crutches for a few weeks. The doctor thought that I had only pulled something, so it did not stop my training or water polo, either. I kept right on doing what I had been, but with the addition of a knee brace.

But my knee injury wasn't the only problem. By the third week in May, Tennie wanted to call off the swim because of my knee, money, and her lack of time commitment. I still wanted to make the swim, but would not be able to do it. There simply was not enough money. I had to face the facts. For two months, it had looked like a reality, but now my dream had slipped away from me again. The dream was no longer possible.

I did not give up hope, though. I continued to train for the swim marathon. On June 9, at 8:00 a.m., I started the swim. Gary and his family and Tennie and my family were there to cheer me on. In five hours and thirty-seven minutes, I completed the swim. Unfortunately, only a little over three hundred dollars was raised for the English Channel swimming fund.

My freshman year was finally over. I wanted to go home. As I drove away from Pomona with my parents, I thought of all my recent experiences. In one year I had gained fifteen pounds, hurt my knee and ankle, fell in love, made many friends from all over the United States, and learned so much, not only in my classes. As Los Angeles disappeared behind us, I wondered if each year would be as interesting and fulfilling.

For the summer, I stayed at my parent's house in San Mateo. I planned on swimming with Foothill and qualifying for the Senior Outdoor Nationals. At the same time I was going to take two physics courses at the local college since I was hoping to major in Physical Education at Pomona in conjunction with a History major.

On our way home from Pomona, we stopped briefly at Foothill College to check on workout times. As I got out of the car, my knee collapsed under me. Worse, Nort acted very frustrated when he saw me. He could not believe that I had gained so much weight, fifteen pounds in one year! However, he thought I could still make Nationals, but said I would have to train through all of the meets through the end of the season.

I began training, and for two weeks I trained very hard. Unfortunately, there was something wrong with my knee. I was having problems doing flip turns, and after workouts, I could barely walk. Finally, my father insisted I see another specialist. MRIs and CT scans were not yet an option, so I was given an arthogram, a test where dye is injected into the damaged area. After the arthogram, x-rays were taken and read, and the doctor determined I needed an operation. I had torn the posterior horn of the medial meniscus. So, I was in the hospital from July 3 through July 13 due to knee surgery and removal of my wisdom teeth. Not until the end of July, was I able to get back into the water.

I had been in the water for only three days when I heard about the Santa Cruz one-mile pier race. The race was August 3. Even though I was still on crutches, I went. The race consisted of a run into the water, a one-mile swim around the pier, and a run up the beach. We lined up along the beach. As the gun went off signaling the start, everyone began running. I could not run, but slowly I made it to the water, dropped my crutches in the surf, and began swimming. I felt very good for being out of the water for over a month. After a few hundred yards, I caught up to Jenny Wylie, a 1972 Olympian in the 400 Yard Freestyle and a former Santa Clara teammate. As we approached the shore, she stood up and ran up the beach, but I realized I could not stand up. While I tried to figure out what to do, a friend rushed out with my crutches. I could not plant them in the sand; the undertow was too much, as was the slant of the beach. So, I dropped the crutches and let the water push me further up the beach. Finally, I was able to hop across the finish line.

This was my first ocean race. I loved it. I was the second woman and the ninth overall. Right then, I decided I had to try some more races.

On August 10, I swam the annual Healdsburg Race, but I was beaten. After winning four years in a row I was now third. This inspired me to get back into shape and to pursue an open water career. This was going to be my specialty.

Five days later I drove to Los Angeles with a friend who was going to support me. There were ocean races every weekend all along the southern California coast. We planned to be in Los Angeles for eleven days. During this time there were four ocean races, so I convinced my mother that I had to try. I had to see if open water swimming really was for me. She finally gave me permission to go and try.

The first race I intended to swim was at Zuma Beach, two days after we arrived. Each morning we went to the beach to train. I was scared; the waves seemed so big. After all, I am only five foot two. It felt as if they were descending upon me, always knocking me around. In turn, my mind made the waves bigger and stronger than they really were. For my first workout I stayed in about an hour with my friend walking the shore. The water was very clear, too clear. Every once in a while I would see a fish. That, in turn, helped me to pick up my pace. I asked about the fish. I was told not to worry as they were only dogfish, a variety of small shark. I did not need to know that at all.

The race at Zuma began at ten in the morning. The start was on a sharply slanting beach. The waves would rise and then drop straight down. As the race began, I watched as most of the swimmers rushed out through the waves. I waited until the waves crashed and the water surged up the beach. After this I quickly limped into the water.

The water felt good and so did I. When I was swimming along, I began thinking of how far it seemed. It was only a mile and the Channel was at least twenty-two. *I'd better get going.* I did, and ended up doing fairly well.

The next race I had planned to swim was cancelled, but before I left Southern California, I swam one other race, a one-mile at Santa Monica. The night before the race it occurred to me that Lynne Cox, the then world record holder for the English Channel swim, would be there. I couldn't stop thinking about this and could not sleep.

There were eighty-five people in the race. I made sure that I warmed up well. As the race began, I started out slowly. About halfway I passed a very large girl. I thought to myself, *she is moving fairly well through the water.* At the finish I had found out that girl had been Lynne Cox. I met her and we talked for quite some time. She was very nice. Lynne even invited me to train with her on weekends during the school year. When I returned home, that was all I could talk about. I had to get a car so that I could drive to the ocean to train for the Channel. I intended to break the record!

Once school began, I managed to drive out to the ocean a couple of times. The most important excursion was to meet with Lynne in October. At that time, she suggested that if I was going to invest all the money and time necessary to swim the Channel I should attempt the Catalina Channel first. She also thought that some of the longer ocean races might be beneficial. After all, why spend a few thousand dollars to go to England and find out that I did not have what it took to be a marathon swimmer, mainly the mental toughness? I was a very dedicated pool swimmer and had tried various long races. I smiled to myself when I heard this. I knew I could handle any situation. It would be another two years before I experienced the mental pain that Lynne had warned me about. This was the double crossing in 1977. We were sitting on the beach in Long Beach for our talk. It was late afternoon; the beach was deserted. The sun was slowly descending. A cool breeze was blowing from the east, and before us lay Catalina. I had never really seen it before. It would not be the last time I would sit and gaze at it either.

I graciously accepted Lynne's advice. She was one of the warmest people I had ever met. This was one aspect of marathon swimming that I enjoyed. In my experience, most of the people are very thoughtful, warm, and encouraging.

OCEAN CIRCUIT, 1975

With the completion of the 1974 collegiate season, Gary asked me if I wanted to coach the Mt. Baldy Aquatics in Claremont. After I had done this for a few weeks, he offered me a summer teaching job at the college, in addition to continuing with the coaching. Added to this, I would be able to commute to the ocean regularly. Also, I would be able to participate in the ocean circuit, and thus further my knowledge of long-distance swimming.

I invited my mother to spend the summer with me. We lived in Tennies's cottage for a month, and then house sat a professor's home for the remainder of the working season. Each morning I would go to Puddingstone Lake with the senior swimmers of Mt. Baldy. There was a one hundred-yard course which the team used for its long course training since they did not have access to a fifty-meter pool. Three days a week I would swim for an hour and a half without stopping; the other mornings I did the team workouts. After this I went to work. I taught swimming from 9:00 a.m. to 2:00 p.m., lifeguarded until 6:00 p.m., then coached four to twelve year olds until 7:15 p.m. This was my Monday through Friday schedule. My mother would have breakfast ready in the morning and usually brought my lunch to work. At night she always had dinner waiting. She kept me going that summer.

On the weekends I would swim in the ocean races in the mornings and lifeguard in the afternoons. In my little free time I took a half credit class.

Money was an issue. Fortunately, I had been given free suits from Speedo since I was five and through my professional career and all my teams wore Speedo, so all we had to come up with was money for gas, entry fees, and food. Not an easy feat.

The ocean circuit began the first week in July with a half-mile swim around the Huntington Pier. It was a very rough swim because the currents flowed into the pier. If the waves were very big, it was likely that many swimmers would be thrown into the pilings. It was at this meet that I met my future ocean team mates. In April, at a water polo game at Long Beach State, I had met Cindy Cleveland, a marathon swimmer. Now at this meet, she was the first person I saw. She, in turn, introduced me to Syndi Goldenson and John York, her ocean teammates. They were bubbling with enthusiasm for their coach and marathon swimming. I had never heard of an ocean team before this; what they were doing was fascinating.

A few weeks passed before I met their coach, Mrs. Siga Gudmundson Albrecht, who was also the head coach of the Surfside Swim Club, one of the top notch teams in southern California. Siga was a demanding woman, full of energy and enthusiasm. She had been a swimmer, a breast stroker, and had swum the ocean circuit for years. In addition to coaching, she was a marathon runner. She transferred many of the training techniques from her running to swimming. Until I met Siga, I had been doing my own training. She invited me to train with her, if I wanted to become a member of the ocean swim team. I was very interested, but decided not to do so until after the Seal Beach 10-Mile Race, my first marathon. What a mistake!

For this race I had asked three of my co-workers if they would like to paddle for me. They had no experience, but neither did I at the time. I had never gone over two miles in the ocean. The only thing I knew about the race itself was that the starting point was Huntington Pier and the finish was on the north side of the Seal Beach Pier. At no time had I even driven the course! Although I was not sure where to station the paddlers on the beach, I made all of the necessary decisions. Mark Ambord would start, and he would paddle four miles. Then, his sister, Julie, would swim out and switch with him. The third paddler would relieve her at the seven-mile point. Little did I know how ridiculous this plan was! If the swimmers stayed within one hundred yards of the beach and if the beach was straight, this may have worked. Unfortunately, the shore twists and curves so that at times I was over a half mile from shore. If I had followed the shore line, I would have swum an extra few miles.

The race was supposed to begin at 6:00 a.m. but did not get going until 6:30 a.m. due to a light fog which hung over the ocean. As the race began, Mark was doing very well, but I was going too fast, and soon he was having trouble keeping up. He began to drop behind. At the time, I was in third or fourth position. After a few miles Mark stopped completely; he could go no further. I did not know what to do, so I kept swimming. At first I was a little nervous being out there all by myself, but I continued. Then all of a sudden, a lifeguard boat pulled alongside me. Julie and Mark were on board. One of the lifeguards jumped in and began to paddle. After a while he wanted to swim with me, while Mark resumed paddling. However, neither could stay with me. The lifeguard quickly returned to paddling. Earlier in the race, a male swimmer had been rather close to me, but fell behind. Finally, we rounded a jetty, and the pier was only a half mile away. I finished second overall by two minutes in a field of twenty, and was the first female to finish. I was tired, but not exhausted.

My first question was *What had happened?* When Julie saw the swimmers coming, she swam out, but she never saw us. The lifeguard patrol boat picked her up very quickly when they saw Julie in distress. A little while later, it came across Mark flailing in the water. Once they found me, Mark and Julie in turn convinced the lifeguard to paddle. The third paddler, Debbie, never even got in the water. From where she was, she could not even see the swimmers.

After the race, Kelly Lang and Jeff Edwards interviewed me for the *Sunday Show,* a local TV show. It went well. In the afternoon I had to lifeguard, but we closed the pool for a few minutes in order to watch the interview on television.

The significance of the swim was that I had met the challenge, I swam ten miles. It was fun. Finally, I had found something for me. I also knew that I could do better and that I would swim the English Channel. I knew it was possible!

Two weeks after the Seal Beach Race there was a fifteen-mile race at Laguna Beach. I wanted to attempt it. Prior to that race, I decided to train with Siga a few times. My mother and I got up a few days at 4:45 a.m. and drove to Hermosa Beach for a workout. The workout usually consisted of a couple of miles and a few sprints. Each swimmer worked out in the ocean everyday besides swimming in the pool. But more than this, there was a coach working with them, telling them what to do and how to do it. I was really interested in becoming a permanent member of that team. I liked what they were doing even though I was scared to death sometimes.

During one of these trips, something occurred that slowed me down. It was the Tuesday prior to the Laguna Race. While I was swimming in to the beach at the Twenty-Second Street tower at Hermosa Beach, I was hit by a wave. I was slowly learning how to go through the surf, but I hated it. The wave hit me at an angle and bent my body a few different ways. It then proceeded to push me ashore. My back was throbbing; I could not stand up. Siga came running to see if I was all right. I was not, so that afternoon, I went to a doctor. He suggested I stay out of the water for at least a week. As every good athlete would, I followed his advice to the tee. For two days I slept on the floor, took my pain medication, and stayed out of the water. Then I went to the Laguna swim.

It was a beautiful swim. I saw many things while I was in the water: a lone stingray peacefully fluttering by, a jellyfish the size of a football bobbing up and down with the hypnotizing waves, the fog hovering over the sleepy coast, the enormous conglomerations of plastic-looking and slimy-feeling seaweed. I had never had to swim through the latter before, and I never wanted to again.

Siga arranged a paddler for me, Paul Tuttle. She did not want another mishap like the one at Seal Beach. Paul paddled the whole race without any problems. He gave me a slight scare at the beginning, though. About two miles out he jumped off the board. He was cold and wanted to get wet, but I did not know what was going on. All I could think was, *Oh goodness, he has quit, too.* I quickly stopped and asked what was wrong. He peered at me and told me to get going. I was relieved that nothing had happened.

For the first ten miles, I had a very close race on my hands. At the seven-mile mark I was really hurting; I needed something to drink. However, Siga was nowhere in sight. She had all the drink and food on the boat with her. She was going from one swimmer to another to see how they and the paddlers were doing. Paul asked a competitor's crew, who accompanied him in a canoe, if they had something I could have to drink. I was given a cup of hot water with honey in it. After that, I felt much better. As I rounded the ten-mile buoy, the boat Siga was on approached. She asked how everything was going, and if I wanted anything to eat. A glass of lemonade and a few cookies went down fairly well. The other swimmer had dropped behind about one hundred yards. Siga warned that John York was catching up with me. He was not, but she wanted me to think so. I told her "No way," and then took off as fast as I could.

I won the race by over twenty minutes. John was second. Lonny Larson, the competitor who helped me and shared the lead for ten miles, finished, but he had severe hypothermia. His eyes were very glassy and his skin had lost its color. I have never forgotten seeing him struggling to stand and walk out of the surf. It took him a few hours to recover from the hypothermia, and since that swim he has not competed in any other long races. A lack of proper preparation and training can be very detrimental and even deadly.

This race made me even more aware of Siga's knowledge of marathon swimming, and her interest in my swimming meant a lot. Siga was able to give me what I had been searching for—support, knowledge, and experience. I liked her very much; I knew I had found the coach for me. Just as quickly, my respect and admiration were directed towards her. Unfortunately, my mother would struggle with jealously because of my respect for Siga.

One of my most memorable races that summer was the Santa Monica one-mile race. As we lined up for the start, the waves were not very big. At the start, I was standing next to John York. As the gun when off and we started running out, suddenly three, six to ten-foot waves appeared out of nowhere.

Everyone else dove under them. I was not an experienced wave swimmer, and I still could not tell when to go through the waves; they scared me. I tried to dive under the first wave but was too late; it was already breaking. John did the same thing. The wave picked us up and carried us up the beach past Siga and Mom. They began yelling at us to get up and start swimming.

I was in shock. *What had happened? Why were all of these people laughing?* It was not funny. Quickly I jumped up and ran out into the waves again. This time I made it through. I even did pretty well in the race. This is still very funny to think of especially when you consider that within a year the two of us would hold world records for the Catalina Channel Swim.

In the third week of August, I finished working. The Goldenson's, Syndi's parents, invited me to spend the next month with them so I could train in the ocean and complete the ocean circuit. Another reason I moved in with the Goldenson's was that our group was contemplating a swim from Los Angeles to San Diego. With the accompaniment of Lynne Cox and one or two other ocean swimmers we thought we could pull off the swim. We hoped this would help advertise marathon swimming and raise money for our future swims. From the start, we ran into difficulties. For days we searched for a boat or two to accompany us. Hans, Siga's husband, got the verbal assistance of the Los Angeles Lifeguards, but there were still so many things to consider. *Was it safe to swim at night? How could we keep all of the swimmers warm? What about food for all of the paddlers, swimmers, assistants, and crew? How could we cross the harbors? Who would be able to navigate such a swim? What would we do if something happened? How many hours or miles would each swimmer swim? Where would we get the money?*—always the hardest question to answer and the first that needed to be answered.

For over three weeks we tried to work out the details. Finally, all thoughts of attempting the swim were dispelled. Maybe the next year we could raise enough money for the crossings, but deep in our minds we knew that this was the end of that idea for this year!

Many things happened while I stayed at the Goldenson's. One incident occurred that I will never forget. Every time I think of it I start laughing. My objective was to train for the La Jolla one-mile swim, only two weeks away. After that I could play.

Our training for the race involved daily workouts in the ocean. I was still very apprehensive to work out without a walker. A walker is someone who keeps a walking pace on the beach with the swimmer, and if anything happened, they would call a lifeguard. It was not until the summer of 1977 that I felt secure without one, well sort of.

One morning, it was very foggy so Syndi and I decided to wait a few hours before we did our workout. Before we knew it, it was late afternoon. We could not miss a workout; Siga would have been irate. So, at four o'clock we went down to do our practice. We had to swim from Hermosa Pier to Manhattan Beach Pier and back, a mere four miles. By the time I had gone three quarters of a mile I was about 250 yards in front of Syndi. I was swimming casually and happened to look towards the bottom. There were a couple of small sharks below me. Not being a fish lover, I stopped to look around to see if anyone was on the beach. There was not. The wind was picking up and the sea was getting choppier. I decided to swim a little faster, and hopefully, I would leave the sharks behind.

For over 200 yards I did not look down. Actually, I did not even open my eyes. Whether it was curiosity or sheer stupidity which enticed me to look downward, I cannot say, but look I did. They were still there. I started to get nervous. I went another 200 yards, but at a much faster pace. A quick peek, and that was it. They were too close. *What was going on?* Here I was out in the ocean by myself, and no one was around except Syndi, who was about a half-mile behind me. I could die and no one would know. With all of the speed I could muster, I sprinted into shore. For a second, I sat down to gather my thoughts. *Syndi . . . she is still out there. I have to go get her before the sharks do.*

I ran down the beach, a miracle in itself, and sprinted out to Syndi. With a panic-stricken voice I told her about the sharks. She knew.

There were three under her. I screamed. We looked at each other and burst into laughter. All the while we were drifting towards the shore. Finally, we started to regain our confidence. At this crucial moment Syndi's foot touched the bottom. She screamed and I jumped on top of her, screaming with all my might. Instinctively, we swam as fast as we could and then both ran up the beach. We ran through the waves and flopped in the sand. As we turned and looked at each other, we burst into laughter. It was so stupid, but neither of us had the courage to get back in.

Instead we went to Siga's and told her what happened. She tried to take it seriously, but she also thought it was funny. Siga knew they were only one to two-foot sharks that would not harm us, but to make us feel better she called the lifeguards. By then our imagination had made them four foot.

The season finished with the La Jolla one-mile race. There were over three hundred and fifty swimmers in various categories. The swim was divided into separate heats. Five minutes ahead of us were the men from twelve to twenty-four. Within a few minutes after the start, I began passing the slower men. It was so crowded. Hans was paddling for me, but he had problems and had to stop. Then I lost my goggles; the race was a disaster. I had passed the third buoy when a lifeguard caught up with me and sent me in the right direction. I was the fifth woman overall and the third in my age bracket. It was a discouraging way to end a successful season.

Another experience I was introduced to was night swimming. One evening Syndi, Siga, and I went for a run on the beach. We watched the sun as it slowly slipped into the sea. As night crept upon us, we went for a dip. It was exciting. I was hit by one small wave after another, though I could not see them. Some fish slithered by also. I really had a good time playing in the surf. Little did I know then about all of the nights that I would train and swim in the darkness.

For coaching us, we presented Siga with a one hundred dollar bill which we had buried in an ice cream container. All that time for only one hundred dollars! She had not asked for anything, but she had given each of us so much. And that was just the beginning.

THIRD SEASON AT POMONA COLLEGE

I n late September 1975, I returned to Pomona College for my junior year. My immediate goal was to qualify for the Women's Nationals in Florida. At the same time, I started thinking about my marathon career. After doing so well in the ten and fifteen-mile races, I decided to swim the Catalina Channel the following summer. I knew I could make it. Besides, I knew it would be a stepping-stone for the English Channel.

Siga sent me a letter in October requesting my presence at a team meeting in November. At the meeting we would be discussing our goals for the following summer. At first the letter threw me for a loop. It was addressed to Penny Bodean. *Bodean, where did she get that?* I had known her most of the summer and she did not even know my last name. I promised myself that she and everyone else would never forget my name. As for Bodean, it remained as a nickname and a constant joke within our close-knit group.

At the meeting, I made the commitment to swim the Catalina Channel. Siga also asked me to make a commitment to a regular schedule of pre-season workouts. The purpose of these workouts would be to become acclimatized to the ocean under different conditions and in different seasons. These included cold water, freezing water, rain, storms, fog, and rough seas, all of which emerged as the warm summer season disappeared. The workouts would be held every weekend. In the beginning they would not be very long. As the year progressed, the mileage and the number of workouts per week would increase.

I could not make a commitment to attend these workouts. I had borrowed my mother's VW Bug so that I could attend as many workouts as possible, but my attendance would depend on my academics. I would attend whenever it was academically possible. Siga accepted that, but stressed the importance of the workouts. She also reaffirmed the old dictum that the training was more important than my social life, especially if I wanted to go after the Catalina record.

It was at this first meeting, before anything was done with regards to the swim, that Siga told us no parents would be allowed on their own child's crossing. This took me by surprise, and I knew that would create problems in my home, especially with my mother. However, if I was going to have Siga as my coach, then it would be this way. I accepted it, and my mother would just have to accept it.

In November I was able to go to the ocean twice. At the second of these, Siga told me about a Christmas clinic at Lakewood Aquatic Club. She had been an assistant coach there since she retired from Surfside in September. She wanted us to attend so that we could improve our techniques and our pool swimming. It would also present us with an opportunity to train in the ocean as a group.

Pool swimming was a significant aspect of Siga's and my training philosophy for marathon swimming. The development of speed is essential to success. That belief had not been maintained by other marathon swimmers or coaches before. If one wanted to maintain a quick but efficient stroke turnover, it is important. That was a key to our success: lots of speed work combined with great quantities of mileage, never losing an efficient stroke or turnover.

Similarly, Siga did not believe in extra bulk to protect against the cold. She did not believe that it would help. Rather, she maintained that it would tend to slow the swimmer down because of the extra resistance. Our body weight was kept as close as possible to our ideal weight for pool competition. Again, this belief was contrary to that of past marathon champions. Siga's philosophy, and gradually our beliefs, were not confirmed until our successes in the summer of 1976 and then reaffirmed in 1977.

As for the clinic, I knew it would be very beneficial for my collegiate season as well. I still had not qualified for the AIAW Women's Collegiate Nationals. The time standard was seven seconds faster than my best time, but I wanted to go to Florida, to the Division I AIAWs.

I decided to go to the clinic. It would give me the opportunity to meet Lakewood Aquatic coach and Olympic coach, Jim Montrella, and train with some top national swimmers again. Besides, I did not know where I would train if I went home. I had not been home for over a year. I could still drive to Foothill, but it would not be the same without Nort who had become the head coach at UC Berkeley. My mother was not too excited about me being away for Christmas, but she realized that it was the best thing for me. Reluctantly, she said it was all right for me to go.

The clinic was excellent. It lasted from 7:00 a.m. to 5:00 p.m. each day. During the day there were three training sessions, films, lectures, and discussions on some aspect of swimming.

From the first moment I met Jim, I was totally impressed. He wanted us to learn about ourselves, our training, everything. He was not trying to produce robots, but, rather, swimmers who were able to understand what they were doing, how they were doing it, and why. Jim was always asking questions. He yelled, screamed, jumped around; always trying to make us think. He cared about each one of us. Within one week I knew I had to continue training with him. Jim had revitalized my interest in pool swimming.

In the second week of the clinic I came down with an ear infection. Whether it was from the pool, the ocean, or overwork, I do not know. It was very frustrating, though. Because of it, I missed the second half of the clinic, and after a few days, I drove home. I spent the next week studying and talking with my mom, and I decided to join Lakewood Aquatic Club (LAC) when I returned to LA. I planned to commute to the Club every weekend so I could train in the pool once or twice, and swim in the ocean.

Upon returning to Pomona, I spoke with Siga about my decision. She was very enthusiastic and said I could stay with her and Hans. The next week I began the first of many weekend excursions. If I did not have a collegiate meet, I would leave school after class on Thursday and return on Monday morning. During that time I was able to attend five LAC workouts and two ocean workouts.

It was very hard, though. I would work out Thursday night until 7:30 p.m. then drive a half hour to Siga's. Quickly, I would eat dinner and then go to bed so I could get up at 5:15 a.m. for morning workout. After workouts I would eat something and then go to the library to study. In the afternoon, I would return for another workout then go back to Siga's. On Saturday and Sunday I would train in the ocean in the morning and study all day. Late Sunday afternoon I would attend the LAC training. On Monday, after morning workout, I would drive the hour back to Pomona College.

Many times I felt as if I were intruding on Siga's and Han's privacy. Sometimes I went to stay with other friends, the Cleveland's or the Goldenson's, but I never really felt at ease anywhere. They were all very wonderful, hospitable and I enjoyed their company, but I still felt I needed my own place.

I eventually qualified for the AIAW Nationals in the 500 yard free, and once at the Nationals posted a lifetime best in the event. While at Nationals, I celebrated my twenty-first birthday. I went water skiing in the Fort Lauderdale canals, and then I took a few weeks off before returning to the ocean. A great way to commemorate all I had learned and accomplished in the past year!

PREPARATION FOR THE CATALINA SWIM

U pon returning from Nationals March, 1976, I needed a few weeks without any training before beginning my summer preparations. After two weeks I went to my first ocean workout. The morning was very foggy and cold and the waves were big, maybe six or seven feet high. It took Syndi and me over twenty minutes to get out beyond the surf where we could swim. Every few seconds another wave would come rushing towards us. We just had enough time to catch our breath before we had to dive under the next wave. By the time we were beyond the waves, we were exhausted. Our swim to the pier and back was nothing compared to the ordeal we had just gone through. As we finished our swim and turned to go back in to the shore, I told Syndi I would rather wait for the rescue boat to come get me. She agreed. However, there was a lull in the waves, so we sprinted in before the next set could run us down. The next morning, I found it was a little hard to force myself to return to the ocean. After being out so long, it was very difficult to adjust to the ocean again.

At the end of April, I began devoting all of my free time to swim and prepare for the Catalina Channel. I found an apartment in Lakewood so I could commute to campus on Monday evenings, stay until Tuesday afternoon, and go back again on Thursdays. I spent little time on campus, giving me more training time at the beach. This extra ocean training helped me prepare for the Catalina swim.

With the conclusion of my junior year, I jumped into a strenuous training program consisting of both ocean and pool workouts daily. The ocean training was very hard to adjust to, however. The previous summer, I had never trained more than five miles in a workout, and now I was expected to do that and much more. Furthermore, I was not used to training in the ocean every day.

The second Saturday in June, John, Cindy, and I went on a one-day excursion with Siga and Hans. We drove to a beach north of Zuma, where we trained, lay in the sun, and had a barbecue. The main purpose of the outing, however, was to discuss the summer and our planned crossings. It would be a long, hard, uphill climb and I knew it. Nevertheless, I wanted to do it and was up to the challenge.

One of the most difficult situations that summer was the hardships suffered by our teammate, Syndi Goldenson. At the end of the previous summer she had been troubled with an ulcer. Then in March she destroyed her knee and had to have an operation on it. Complications resulted, and she developed a few blood clots. For a while, she really had it rough. Her dream to swim Catalina had to be postponed. She, and the rest of us, hoped this was only temporary. That summer she did a lot for each of us. None of our crossings would have been as successful without her. I owe her more than I could ever say. She is a good friend!

After three weeks of training, I was beginning to adjust to the pace and the demands of the training schedule, but then I developed an ear infection and had to stay out of the water for a few days. Again, I wondered: *Why was this happening? Was it mental?* Although I was sidelined for only a short while, I was becoming very frustrated, and feared that at that rate, I would never be ready for the Catalina Channel.

My training schedule was extremely hectic. On Monday, Wednesday, and Friday I trained from 6:00 to 9:00 a.m. with LAC in the pool. Then I would drive twenty minutes to the ocean and swim from ten in the morning until two or three in the afternoon. After each workout, we would meet to discuss our times, strokes, upcoming meets, or anything else that had to be arranged. By the time I returned home, it was four o'clock. Usually I would then take a nap for an hour or two because I was so tired.

Tuesday and Thursday were tougher. After my morning swim, I returned to the apartment to rest for a while. Then, at 11:30 a.m., I would head to the ocean for a workout from noon until 3:00 or 3:30 p.m. On those days, we worked on developing our speed and improving our ins and outs. We also sought to experience a variety of swimming environments, so we would travel to different beaches. After these workouts ended, I'd head home. After an hour's nap, I would return to the pool for an evening workout with LAC which usually lasted from 6:00 to 7:30 p.m.

By the time the weekend rolled around, I did not want to do anything. I was spent and wanted to recoup. Of course this wasn't to be: there was always a Saturday workout and often a meet to attend. Sunday was my day off. Most Sundays I just wanted to loaf around and not go anywhere. My favorite activity on my day off was watching a movie and eating chocolate or ice cream. Sunday became a real reward to the soul day!

My mother spent that summer with me. Like all parents and children, we had our conflicts, and this summer was no exception for us. When the management raised the rent on our apartment ten dollars a month, Mom left the heat on and the hot water running all day and night. Also, she turned on the oven and the burners and left them on for hours. Her goal was to get more than her ten dollars back. It drove me a bit crazy, but that was my mom. The saving grace with my mother was that she enjoyed the beach. After attending community college for the day, she liked to come down to the beach. She'd walk the beach with me or speak with Siga. Walking the beach helped me swim faster. I would try to keep up with her. If she didn't walk, she spoke with Siga about my swimming. Both helped my swimming. I appreciated her being there, especially when she walked with me and what she did for me. Siga couldn't walk with each of us, so this helped a lot.

The training was very difficult, especially from a mental standpoint. At times I had no energy or desire to continue. By mid-July, my stroke was not feeling as strong as it should be, and I was concerned. That summer I also developed a desire to make the AAU Nationals in the 1500 meters, besides breaking the record for the Catalina Channel. Siga and Jim were supportive of my goals because they thought it was possible and they did not want to discourage me. In retrospect, it would have been better if they had. I went on a short taper, but overall I did not do well; I did not qualify.

So, my pool competition ended for awhile. My thoughts and efforts would now be directed to the most important challenge—the Catalina Channel. I intended to break the record for swimming from the mainland to Catalina. The record was eight hours thirty two minutes by Lynne Cox. I wanted to swim it in under eight hours. Siga constantly reminded me that the conditions would be the determining factor. Nevertheless, I continued to nurture my goal.

Throughout the summer we would often work at Seal Beach. We would arrive at our main training beach just as Dave Cox's team was leaving. His team consisted of Pat Slupe, David Yudovin, Dan Slosberg, Lynne and Ruth Cox. The first two would also be attempting the Catalina channel in mid-August. Pat was fast. Both he and Dave felt they were faster than me. They would have to wait and see.

On the Tuesday before the race I did a mile warm up as Pat was finishing his workout. Soon, we began racing, and by the end of the mile, we were sprinting. This was the first time Pat realized that I would give him a race. Little did he know I was playing with him. The Seal Beach 10-Mile would dispel any feelings of superiority on his part.

At the end of July, I competed in the Huntington to Seal Beach 10-Mile. At Seal Beach, I surprised a few swimmers. I was first, the overall winner by twenty minutes. The time of the swim was slower than the year before, mainly due to opposing currents. This frustrated me immensely. Siga's warning had proven correct, even though it had not sunk in, and would not for another year.

ONE MONTH TO GO

T he weekend following Seal Beach the first annual Catalina
Classic, a fifteen-mile race, was held, jointly sponsored by Siga
Albrecht and Dave Cox, the only other marathon coach in
Southern California. The Classic started at the Isthmus and swam south
to Avalon, hugging the coast. Since both coaches wanted to further
marathon swimming and had swimmers attempting the Catalina
Channel, they felt another long race would be beneficial. Furthermore,
the Laguna fifteen-mile race had been reduced to only an eight-mile
race.

Siga and Dave worked very well together, as did the two groups.
Together with some help from the chairman of marathon swimming,
Richard Yeo, the swim was organized. Remembering the extreme
exhaustion and resultant hypothermia of the swimmer at the Laguna
fifteen-mile the previous year, the coaches decided to require proof
of completion of a ten-mile swim. Although that would limit the
competition, they hoped it would ensure that all the swimmers had
the necessary experience to protect them from suffering any ill effects
from this swim.

The race was fifteen miles from the Isthmus near the north end of
the Catalina Island to Avalon at the south end. It would begin at the

dock at the Isthmus and conclude at the main beach in Avalon, just east of the harbor.

A few days prior to the swim, it seemed to me that the race was very disorganized, and that no one knew what was going on. This made it very difficult to make arrangements for paddlers and transportation. Also, too many things were still up in the air. However, neither of the coaches expressed any concern, and instead indicated that they did not feel that we needed to know all the details ahead of time. After all, besides our two teams, there would be only two other competitors. At twenty-one, and a bit of a perfectionist, I liked to know everything that was happening. Also, I had to explain all the details to my mother who was asking numerous questions daily. This created quite a bit of stress for me.

As it turned out, we had the option of sailing over on the steamer in the afternoon or flying over earlier that morning. Not being an enthusiastic sailor, I decided to fly over. This would allow me time to set up camp. I would have preferred to sleep in a motel the night before the race because I never slept very much when I went camping, but those were the best sleeping arrangements that could be made.

As I figured out the costs of the swim which included the five dollar entry fee, transportation (either ten dollars by boat or twenty-five dollars by plane), the food for two days (approximately fifteen dollars), and odds and ends of at least another five dollars, I could not believe the expenses involved. The least figure amount was thirty-five dollars and the maximum fifty dollars. (Compared to similar swims today, this was nothing.) It was expensive, but beneficial to my crossing, since I would encounter not only different water temperatures but more sea life that I was used to seeing. I firmed up my plans to go by plane with John.

John and I flew over on Friday morning. Initially, we set up camp then explored the island a bit, after our workout of course! After we watched everyone else arrive by boat, we all returned to the camp.

With the late afternoon sunlight creeping over my shoulders, I glanced towards the mainland. Throughout the morning it had been too overcast to see the mainland, but with the afternoon breeze, the Catalina Channel was now visible. This was the first time I had seen the Catalina Channel from that direction. Quietly, I left the camp for a better vantage point. Nestled on a rock, high upon a hillside overlooking our campsite in the harbor, I sat mesmerized by the Channel. I peered at the undulating, clear blue water that served as a barrier between the island and the mainland and contemplated my upcoming challenge. In a month or so I would try to break this barrier and in essence bring the two closer together. Similarly, Pat and Dave would have their chance in only two weeks.

Without realizing how long I had been away, I nonchalantly strolled back into camp. Immediately, I was assailed with questions ("Didn't I know I had been gone nearly an hour?") and outrageous accusations ("You didn't care that we were worried something had happened to you."). Apparently everyone had assumed that I had left because I was in a bad mood since I hadn't told anyone I was leaving and had been gone for quite some time. At first I was infuriated. I had only wanted to be by myself, to ponder the upcoming race and the future. An important aspect of my mental preparation prior to a swim is to go off by myself for an hour or so of peaceful contemplation or to listen to music in a quiet room. This puts me in the right state of mind for a race. I also tend to get very quiet the day before. I had done this before other races, so I didn't think anything of it when I wandered off earlier. I think everyone was worried.

Around 6:00 p.m. we had dinner, then sat around the camp fire and talked for awhile. At 9:00 p.m. a lifeguard drove up while some of us were preparing for bed. The Coast Guard Auxiliaries had arrived with the paddleboards, and they had to be unloaded right away. For safety reasons, the boards could not be left at the pier. Since it would be nearly impossible to carry them to the campsite, the lifeguard had told the Auxiliaries to unload them by the water just below our camp. However, there was not a dock or any lights on the shore. Off everyone went, walking down the dark path to the water's edge. It was so hard to see. *Which boats were the Auxiliaries?* None of the nearby vessels had lights on them or were making any noise. After a few minutes a few brave volunteers, the paddlers, entered the water and tried to locate the boats. They searched in vain for half an hour, when finally they located the boats. Slowly the transfer began. In the meantime, all the swimmers were sent to bed. We were just falling asleep as this cold and tired party returned from their completed expedition. Immediately the fire was rekindled, lighting the whole area. For nearly an hour they stood around warming themselves and exchanging stories. I could not sleep through all of the commotion, and started to get nervous about the race. Finally, I fell asleep only to be awakened when the last few swimmers arrived at 11:30 p.m. on the *Catalina Cruiser*. With their arrival came more noise and confusion, and as a result, I spent a restless night getting little sleep.

The darkness slipped away at 5:30 a.m. Slowly, and with little enjoyment, we crawled out of our warm sleeping bags to a very brisk morning. Quickly we fixed something to eat, then began breaking camp. Once done, we started our long trudge back to the Isthmus, but all the hurrying was in vain. The race would not begin for over an hour and a half. The boats had to be brought in, loaded, and assigned to the various groups (boats, paddlers, and swimmers). The final details of the swim were completed as we stood around anxiously awaiting the start.

At 8:00 a.m. the race finally began. As we swam through the harbor, I quickly pulled ahead, never to be challenged again in the race. My stroke felt a lot better than it had in any other race that summer. The swim was very difficult, though. During the swim I encountered some rough swells, but more than that, I was continuously being stung by miniscule jellyfish. There were thousands of them, and it was impossible to avoid them. Similarly, the paddlers' hands were burning with pain as their hands were being stung also.

That week had been our longest with regard to mileage, too. One day, we had swum twelve miles straight. To be racing fifteen miles made us nervous.

As the race wore on, I became very tired. I wanted to stop for ERG, electrolyte replacement of glucose, more often than I had ever before. Beyond that, I wanted to speak with my paddler, Hans, because I needed his reassurance. The swim was very monotonous. At one point, the boat with Siga and Dave aboard came near me to see how we were doing. Jokingly, Dave waved a bag of M&M Peanuts at me. If I swam to the boat, I could have them. He was trying to induce me to slow down so that Dave and Pat who were one mile behind, could catch up. Unsuccessfully, Siga tried to conceal them from my sight. She also attempted to steal the bag of M&Ms from Dave, and for a second I thought she might fall into the water. It was funny to watch, but I pretended to ignore it. As I began swimming again, I abruptly turned in the direction of the boat, and sprinted towards it. Hans and everyone on the boat started yelling. After a minute or two of excitement and fun, I just as abruptly returned to my original course and waved goodbye to them.

The last few miles were exasperating. I thought I would never finish. At long last I entered the harbor. Thinking I was almost finished, I sprinted. Much to my amazement, however, the harbor went on and on for almost a mile. Then after a quick turn, the beach was only 200 yards in front of me. Siga was waiting for Hans and me at the finish. There were many people in the water and more lying in the sun. Upon finishing, the first thing Hans and I wanted was a bag of peanut M&Ms. Damn! They had been left on the boat! It had stopped just long enough to drop off Siga, then left to return to the course to follow the other swimmers. To make matters worse, all of our clothes, food, and money had been put on the wrong boat. Fortunately, some people loaned us their towels, and the sun warmed us up nicely, so we did not freeze. While we relaxed, Hans borrowed some money and found a bag of M&Ms, which we quickly devoured.

While waiting for the others to finish, Siga and I discussed the race. It had seemed so long. For the Catalina Channel, I would have another five or six miles, yet at the end of this race I was physically and mentally exhausted. Could I still make the Catalina Channel? Siga told me not to worry; I could, and in record time. She was very pleased with my swim today. She knew Catalina would be a hard swim, and that was why this swim had been important to do. She felt that I needed to experience the pain that I would encounter on the crossing.

Within half an hour Dan finished, with John only a few hundred yards behind him. Over two hours later, Cindy Cleveland also completed the swim.

As we anxiously awaited her arrival, a local promoter approached us. He was very upset with us because he had not been informed about the race. He said he could have given the race a lot of publicity. He then proceeded to take numerous pictures of the group, swimmers, paddlers, and coaches while he told us of a project he was working on. This project was to organize a 50th anniversary celebration of the 1927 Catalina crossing. In that race, 102 contestants swam but only one succeeded, seventeen-year-old George Young of Canada. For his win, Young received $25,000. The promoter wanted to have a similar swim for $25,000. Naturally, I was very interested. He was disappointed when he learned that I and the others would be doing a crossing that summer, as he felt that we should wait until January and do it on the date of the 1927 swim. Nevertheless, he offered to do all the publicity for the swims. As soon as Cindy completed the race, a brief award ceremony was held, so it was 5:00 p.m. before I was able to leave the island. As for the Catalina Channel, all I could think now was how far fifteen miles felt. It had been a long weekend; I was tired.

With the coming of August, the Island was visible every day. Prior to that time, I had not seen it during a single workout all summer. Now, with the swim fast approaching, the Island became a constant reminder of my next challenge.

On August 5, four of us went out in the mid-channel with pilot Mickey Pittman on the *Bandido* to swim part of the route I would follow in the race. Since I knew I would get seasick, I only had a cup of tea and a piece of toast for breakfast. As I was training, I did not take any seasick medication. At the beginning, everything went well. However, once the boat left the calm waters of the harbor, we encountered very high swells, and much to my discomfort, the boat headed directly into them. At first I tried not to think about it, so I went aft. Not feeling much relief, I joined Siga in the cabin. She was not feeling very well, either. Tightly, we clutched each other and commiserated over our predicament. We stayed this way until we reached our destination, seven miles off the coast, opposite Marineland.

After an hour of suffering, the boat slowed to circle the seven-mile buoy. My instinct was to jump into the water but unfortunately, I would have to go below and put on my suit. So, off I went. The ship was rocking miserably with each passing wave, and upon my ascent to the deck, I knew I could not hold my food any longer. Quickly, I leaned over the side rail and relieved myself of everything inside me. Still feeling a little queasy, I threw myself in the water. It had to be better in the water! For the first ten minutes or so I was still miserable, but gradually the water transformed me into a dolphin gliding through the water.

Feeling similar, Siga, too, wanted to get off the boat. However, she and Dave decided to accompany us in the rowboat, but soon they were unable to keep up. In a few minutes, they were a few hundred yards behind us and drifting way off course. Mickey turned the boat around and proceeded to pick them up. We swam for about five miles. At times, I was very confident I had the courage to sprint in front of the group, yet at other times I became frightened and wanted the security of the boat. The closer we got to Marineland, the colder the water became. This was due to the upwelling currents off of the continental shelf. Approximately a mile from Marineland, we left the water and climbed back into the boat. The boat continued towards a point, so that we could see where each of us would finish, or, in my case, where I would start.

After the training, I felt a lot better, and so did everyone else. My stomach had settled down, my head was no longer throbbing. Adding to the relief, the sun had broken through the early morning clouds which had been hanging over us. It was a beautiful day. The boat peacefully returned to port while we lounged on the forward deck. Cheerfully, we reminisced about the long summer that was finally coming to an end. After setting the course, Mickey joined us on deck. He confirmed the final date for swims. My swim was scheduled for Wednesday, September 1, at approximately 12:01 a.m.

There was only one other type of situation that Siga felt we needed to experience before our crossing. This was night swimming. Obviously this was of vital importance since the majority of the swim would occur at night. So, we had night workouts on three separate occasions in the next two and a half weeks. At the first session, I was very apprehensive. To alleviate this tension, both of the teams trained together. Six swimmers came the first time, so we were divided into three groups of two as a safety precaution. Dave conducted the workout that evening. Carrying a lantern, he walked the beach with us. For the first half mile, we crowded together and attempted to swim through the surf line in knee-deep water. After overcoming our initial fears, we gradually dispersed into our predetermined groups and moved into deeper water.

It was a mystifying experience. The luminous full moon permeated the dark sky and created an eerie fluorescent effect in the water. The bubbles glittered as if they were jewels protruding in an aqueous solution. The water seemed to ooze around my arms as I meticulously stroked. A feeling of calmness slowly came over me, and when I emerged from the water, I was in a peaceful mood. The training had been very worthwhile. Similarly, the other night workouts went as well. In addition, on these occasions, Hans paddled with us. This aided in our adjustment to guiding off of a paddler in the darkness. Unfortunately, despite these night practices, I still shivered with fright whenever I unexpectedly saw the black skag of Han's paddleboard. It looks like an underwater shark swimming nearby me.

In the middle of August, I won the last long race of the summer, the Laguna eight-mile swim. It had been reduced from fifteen miles of the year before. After a twenty-minute break, I swam the three-mile race and won that also. I was pleased to have won the speed and endurance race this year, also. Throughout the season I was not beaten by a male or female in any race over three miles, and I was never beaten by a woman in any race. With the completion of these races, I had only one more meet prior to my crossing.

On August 16, I stopped training in the pool. It was sixteen days before my swim, and it was also the week of Pat and Dave's crossing. Both planned to swim from Catalina to the mainland since this was the direction of the fastest men's record. Coincidentally, the current men's record was eight hours fifty minutes, set by their coach, Dave Cox, in 1974. Pat would be going first, as he had a very good chance of the record. Dave Cox had invited Siga along so she could observe the swim firsthand which would help her on our crossings. She was curious how a swimmer would react under pressure, as well as how

Dave and the navigator would handle the various situations that could arise. Pat's swim, however, was far from ordinary. After being in the water for only an hour and a half, he quit. Without saying a word, he disqualified himself by climbing onto the paddler's board. He had felt poorly the whole way, and just could not face another seven or eight hours of excruciating pain. It was not worth it to him. Mentally, he was not ready. Once he gave up mentally, there was little he could do to help himself. Perhaps what was most discouraging was that he did not give anyone else the chance to help him, either.

Despite Pat's failure, Dave Yudovin had an excellent swim the next day. He had less swimming experience than the rest of us, but his determination made up for any lack of expertise. The swim inspired and reignited the rest of us, who were in a daze over Pat's failed swim.

Dave's swim gave me a lot of confidence. Our team trained by swimming twice as far all summer, and I knew it would pay off. I was ready. All I had to do was wait. With each passing day, my mileage dropped more and more.

As with most races, the cost to participate can often prevent a competitor from participating. Wanting to ensure that I could manage the expenses that would be associated with the Channel swim, I had another swim marathon in May to raise the money for the swim. I only swam 500 lengths, but I raised a little over $500. Combined with the money that was left from my first marathon, I would be able to pay for the whole swim in September. The expenses would include the $500 navigator's fee, food for me and the crew for the swim, and all the equipment needed, such as suits, goggles, caps, and squeeze bottles.

One of the things worth noting is that on the crossing outside of the navigator and his crew, all the people were volunteers. This meant that many of them had taken time off from work or school to be there. On each swim there had to be at least three official timers, at least three paddlers, and one or two other people to help with arrangements. The swim would not have been possible without their help, dedication, and enthusiasm. I am truly indebted to all these people who made my swims successful.

CATALINA HERE I COME

Three days before my swim on Sunday, August 29, 1976, I moved in with Siga. She wanted to make sure that I would not be bombarded with questions from anyone, including my family, newspaper reporters, or friends. She just wanted me to relax. Furthermore, she did not want me to think about my swim.

The day before I went to Siga's, my father, younger brother, and his girlfriend Kelly Stanton, came to spend some time with me. My older sister would arrive the day of the swim. After some discussion, it was decided that the following day we would go to Tijuana, spend the day shopping, then on the way back, they would drop me off at Siga's home.

The next morning, after an easy two-mile swim, we left for Mexico. We spent the whole day shopping and talking, and did not return until the late afternoon. At Siga's, I said goodbye to my family, knowing I wouldn't see them again until the morning of my swim. I was excited, but nervous as we parted.

During the three days I spent at Siga and Hans', my upcoming swim was rarely discussed. They handled all the last-minute details while I sat around attempting not to think about my swim. Every time I sat down, disappeared a second, or stopped talking, Siga would ask me what I was doing. She did not want me to think, and was vigilant in her efforts to ensure I that didn't.

She tenaciously screened my conversations while I stayed at her house. She wanted to ensure that no one psyched me out. Physically, I was prepared to swim the Catalina Channel in July, but at the time I lacked the mental preparation that was so very important for such an undertaking. In marathon swimming, more than in any other sport, the mental attitude is at least 85 percent of the battle.

At one point I questioned how much pain, isolation, and stress I could take. *What if I gave up?* Siga was attempting to keep the physical and mental components of the crossing separate, and she did a very good job. Not until four hours before the swim did we discuss any details, including who was paddling for me. (After the swim, I learned that two of my paddlers had had problems and been unable to go on the swim. I never knew there had been any conflict.)

The evening before the swim, I realized that the essential aspect of the swim was the struggle. The Olympic motto similarly attests to this, "The most important thing in the Olympic Games is not to win but to take part, just as the most important thing in life is not the triumph but the struggle, the essential thing is to have fought well." Paralleling this thought, Don Juan in *A Separate Reality*, maintains that a warrior does not care whether he wins or loses, he only cares about the struggle. Athletics, whether it involves an individual or a team, presents the athlete with an opportunity to pit himself against his opponents. The opponent may be a person, a physical object such as a clock, a mountain, a shark, an ocean or even himself. Personally, I believe the most demanding challenge is the struggle against oneself: the struggle between physical pain and mental exhaustion. Superficially, I could say I challenged the Catalina Channel or that I was trying to break Lynne Cox's record, but I know this was not the real challenge. The real challenge came from within. I was struggling with and against myself. On September 1, I would have to face this challenge.

The morning before my swim, Siga and I drove to Lakewood for a brief visit with my family. This was hard as they wanted to spend more time with me, particularly my mother who thought I was old enough to do so. She was jealous and unable to always understand the importance of a calm mental state before a marathon swim, although she was worried about the swim. Siga was concerned that my mother might say or do something which would interfere with my concentration or confidence. Fortunately, peace reigned.

After the visit, we returned to Siga's for the rest of the day. I listened to music and spoke with Siga and Syndi Goldenson. Gradually the day slipped into evening. We had pancakes for dinner. It was really hard to force myself to eat them, but I did. They were good; I just wasn't hungry. About 7:00 p.m. Hans left for the boat.

Night of single crossing, ready to leave Siga's home

At 8:00 p.m. I got dressed, then sat around in my suit watching TV until 9:00 p.m., when Dottie York, John's mother arrived. She had agreed to drive us to Marineland at 10:00 p.m. The swim was scheduled to commence at 12:01 a.m.

During the drive to Marineland I did not even think of my swim. Strangely, I felt very confident. My mental preparation was complete. The eight hours of training a day, the night swimming, the mid-channel swim, and all the successful races had all aided in bringing about this feeling.

A few friends had come for the start: Tennie, Anne Bages (the head of the Physical Education Department at Pomona College), and Major

Bernabe and Captain Margia with some ROTC cadets. Also, present were Mr. Yeo, the head of marathon swimming for Southern California, and Mrs. Cleveland. With all these friends and supporters present, I felt a little more confident and very reassured.

As I stood on the rocks with only my Speedo suit, cap, and goggles on, I noticed how peaceful it was out there. The only sound was that of the waves crashing on the rocks. I stared at the water as it rhythmically rushed madly towards my feet then quickly receded. The water felt comfortable as it undulated over my toes or at least this is what I had programmed myself to believe.

Actually, the water was around 60°. Lynne Cox had warned me that the first hour and a half would be the toughest. One reason for this would be that the water would be colder at the start than during the last fifteen miles of the swim. Therefore, I mentally had prepared for the colder water. I knew that if I could get through the first few minutes in this cold water, I could make it all the way. Another reason would be the initial realization of the distance to be swum. I had swum fifteen miles, but never twenty-one. If I made it through the first five cold miles, I would be set.

Getting ready for single crossing of Catalina

After Siga plastered my body with Vaseline, she was rowed out to the boat which would be at my side throughout the swim. The warning gun would not be sounded until she was on the boat, and everything was set. It seemed like an eternity before I heard the warning blast. My body was shaking out of control. I was not cold nor did I feel nervous, but I was shaking.

As I glanced towards the boat, I thought that it looked really tiny. Then the starting shot was fired. Momentarily, I hesitated; then people began yelling frantically. I could not comprehend what was being said, so I just tuned everything out. Mechanically, I crawled across the slippery rocks into the retreating water. Quickly, I began stroking through the waves. I remember saying to myself, *God, I am actually swimming the Catalina Channel; I have waited so long.*

Immediately, it felt as if I had a fish in my suit. I tried to pull it out, but only got Vaseline on my hand. I was able to grab the fish, and a few seconds later the first two paddlers pulled alongside me. Hans was on my right, but I could not tell who was on the left because he was in the glare of the boat, situated between the boat and me. This did not bother me at the time, but it would lead to a critical situation later. Furthermore, my left goggle was leaking, but I did not want to take the time to clear it. I said hello to the people on the boat, and then attempted to clear my goggles, but I only succeeded in smearing Vaseline all over the outside of the goggles. My goggles problem would have to wait.

It had been planned that I would stop every two hours for an ERG break unless Siga felt I needed it more often. Personally, I believed I needed more breaks, but I never communicated this to Siga. I am not sure why I didn't, except that she was the coach and I deferred to her experience.

At the first break at 2:15 a.m., I listened intently as Siga told me how my stroke was and how far I had gone. I did not have any complaints except that my goggles were still leaking, so another pair was tossed to me immediately. I was pleased with the swim at this point; however, within the next two hours, I would be on the verge of giving up.

One of the problems was that there was not a breeze, so the fumes from the boat hung over the water. After inhaling these for a while, my stomach began to feel upset. To counteract, this I was moved from the right rear of the boat to the right front. I no longer smelled the fumes, but I encountered a new problem: darkness. Up to that point, I had been swimming within the lights of the boat. It was now pitch black.

On the paddleboard to my right a flashlight served as a guiding point. Unfortunately, I was having difficulty seeing it since this particular paddler would pull ahead and then drop back a few strokes behind. Within a few minutes I began running into a one paddler, then the other. Initially, this did not bother me too much, but as the swim wore on, I became aggravated.

Soon, I began to focus on the little things that were happening and started questioning these occurrences and myself. *Why can I not see the people and the boat or the other paddler?* I needed this eye contact.

This was my second mistake, my first being not clearing my goggles well enough. I had done well thus far by not concentrating on the swim, the problems, or the distance I still had to swim. However, once the questioning began, the mental struggle began.

In the next twenty minutes the fumes again became a problem. This time I dropped behind the boat. Gradually I was moved to the left rear, and finally, completely in front of the boat off the left side. It was so dark and lonely. The lights had been rigged for the sides and the back, but now I was ahead of the boat. The lights could not be moved. Worst of all, the paddleboard with the flashlight was on my right side, in the glare of the boat. Even though there was no direct light, there was still a glare. The flashlight could not be switched to the board on the left side because that eye was swollen shut. I began wondering if anything else would go wrong.

The situation was further aggravated when the navigator had to start yelling the directions to the paddlers. They, in turn, had to transfer these orders to me. Considering the fact that I was swimming over three miles an hour, it was very difficult for me to hear everything they said. Furthermore, I was getting tired at this point in the swim. I could not see the boat nor my paddlers, my left eye was shut, and now I had to concentrate on their vocal commands. Prior to the swim, we had worked out various hand signals since I have great difficulty hearing when I swim. Of course, these were to no avail at this point. I began thinking, *What will happen next? Come on relax, everything will work out.* No matter what I tried to think of I could not take my mind off these problems. *I am so tired. No I am not; it is just mental.*

The mental struggle was really getting tough. Physically I was tired, but without the mental support, I would be in trouble. During the next half hour, I ran into one paddler then the other one. All they could do was yell, "Right; left." I remember muttering, *Damn it; make up your mind.* Of course, they were just doing their job, and desperately trying to keep me on course. At the same time, they tried to keep me going mentally. At times I felt as if I were swimming sideways. Once, I was so disorientated, I thought they had turned me completely around and we were heading back towards the mainland! Quickly I lifted my head to see if this was the case. Nothing was visible in all the darkness; I was very frustrated.

At one point, I was even run over by the two paddlers as I could not maneuver as fast as they could. Hans ran over me once too often, so I stopped and glared at him with hatred beaming from my eyes. He knew I was frustrated, but there was nothing he could do. Both paddlers were doing the best they could under these conditions. (As it turned out, it was I who was off course.)

After the swim, I found out that Hans had been fighting with Siga during this time. Everyone was pretty tired and the only one who had remained calm was Siga. She kept telling Hans, "Look, we have to get through this. Try to relax. Just ignore it and keep going." But Hans knew I was having some mental problems and was doing his best to help. He was concerned, particularly after seeing my negative reaction. How much, they could never comprehend, nor would they ever know.

I began dwelling on the fact of how slowly I was swimming. *I must be going too slowly for the record. See I always knew I was a quitter.* Then I remembered the Golden Gate swim, and my thoughts quickly changed. *What about Pomona College? Had I gone there instead of Arizona State because I would be the best swimmer for the women and men? What was wrong with me?* Then my thoughts jumped to musings about the people on the boat. *Don't they know I'm having a problem? Have they all gone to sleep or something? Why have they not moved the lights? They must not care! I might as well stop and rest. It really does not matter anymore. Besides, two hours* must *have gone by. I am hungry and desperately need some ERG. The water is so cold, too.*

At this point, I asked Hans if I could have something to eat. No response. I asked again, still no response. Finally, with tears in my eyes, I stopped briefly and asked Hans for a break. I was crying as I waited for some response. I continued to swim though, intently watching for the stop signal. I was cold. Mentally, I had given in to the pain.

Finally, Hans told me fifteen minutes. *Fifteen minutes; oh shit!* The paddlers were trying to encourage me, but I was not listening. I did not care; I needed some ERG! I was cold and hungry, and at the end of my rope. My turnover slowed considerably, and I could not swim much further, or at least this was what I was telling myself, so I could justify my stop. Yet, I did not want to get out of the water. This I kept out of my mind. I wanted to rest and to talk with Siga in order to get my head together. I needed a break from my negative thoughts and some acknowledgment for what I was doing and how it was going.

Those fifteen minutes seemed like an hour. When I finally stopped, I was shaking continuously. The first and only thing I wanted to know was how far I had gone and what time it was? Hans looked at me and said he did not know; he did not have a watch. Yet I knew he did. When we were planning the race, he had promised not to lie to me. When I reminded him of this fact, he meticulously lifted the sleeve of his wetsuit and said it was 4:15 a.m. A little over four hours had gone by. Immediately my mind was calculating how many miles I should have gone in that time. At the most, I should have swum twelve miles, and at the least, nine and a half miles. Hans said he did not know the exact distance, but gathered it was about seven miles. *Oh my God, only seven miles. I will never make it.* Siga was standing at the back of the boat which was twenty yards in front of us. She yelled that I could not quit now, I had to keep fighting. She did not know that Hans had given me this estimate. I still did not believe that I had swum only seven miles, so I asked her the same question. I watched her quickly walk up to the cabin and talk to the navigator, Mickey Pittman. She was there a few minutes, and when she returned, she told me I had gone eleven miles.

I was ecstatic! At this point I knew I could make it, no matter what else happened. The record was mine, and by a lot. The first thing that came to mind was that I had just given up mentally and was swimming slowly, but that if I took off, I could do anything I wanted. When I finished the ERG, I joyously threw the water bottle back to Hans. He pointedly reminded me to quit feeling sorry for myself and get going. I smiled at him. He knew exactly what I had been doing. I had given in to the mental pain; the physical pain was not as overwhelming as I had mentally let it become. After relieving myself of some extra fluids, I glanced up at Siga. She yelled at me to get going. I took off as fast as I could. I was still cold, but after a few minutes I felt a lot better. It felt awesome!

Everything seemed to go much better from that point. I did as much as possible and kept my spirits high and my pace at 100 percent. For a while I sang patriotic songs and Helen Reddy's *I Am Woman*. Then, some inspirational songs, *Impossible Dream*, and all of Barbra Streisand's songs I could remember. These helped me to fight the ever-increasing pain. I attempted anything to keep me going full speed; not to let up at all as I really wanted it. Concurrently, I thought about people on the boat and how much each was helping me. My main thoughts were of Siga. Throughout the swims, she had remained on the deck, and never took her eyes off me. She was there during all of my swims and for those of my teammates regardless of the hours involved. This gave me a warm feeling. I had to do this for her. She was doing everything for me. Besides Siga, my mother, family, and the Troyers were on the island. I could not get out. Besides, I never wanted to ride on the boat anyway.

I told myself that if something happened and I did not break the record, I had made it through the roughest part. I kept going, and that was the challenge. I had won the battle. Ten minutes earlier I had been on the verge of defeat, I was hurting physically and mentally, and I had begun to give into the struggle. Yet something clicked when I found out how far I had gone. I realized that I was at the turning point of the swim, and in a sense, of my life. I could either quit, or give it everything I had and then some.

I chose the latter. It was as if I was reborn. I am not saying the last three hours were easy, my goodness, every muscle in my body ached, but I was still able to get beyond the pain.

On the second break, I obtained new goggles. These were much better, and my left eye gradually cleared up enough so that near the end of the swim I could even see out of it a little. Furthermore, I was dropped fifty yards behind the boat with the spotlight turned directly on me. This lit the water all around me. It also made me feel warmer and more secure. These changes were very good. The only exception was the fact that the boat was so far in front of us that it prevented any eye contact between Siga and me. I missed that.

In the early morning hours I started to be stung continuously by little jellyfish. Not only did this sting, but it was rather annoying. Soon, in the distance, I could see the Island, although I had no idea how far away it was. It did not matter because as soon as I saw it, I started to sprint. Little did I know that I was over five miles from the shore. It looked so close.

At 6:15 a.m. I had my third break. However, the boat was too far ahead for me to talk with Siga. Neither of my paddlers, Paul or Dan, knew what time it was nor how far we were from the shore. Dan switched sides with Paul and started encouraging me intensely. I tried to push it even harder. I never felt so much pain, but I thrived on it. The more pain, the more I pushed myself.

As it started to get lighter outside, I began wondering what time it was. After a while Hans replaced Dan on the boat which now sat about twenty-five yards off to my left. With a foot-wide smile, Hans held up one finger and yelled, "One more mile." That last mile seemed to take a long time. Hans was calling off the yardage with each stroke I took. The closer we were to the Island, the more the water was infested with jellyfish, and the more I was stung. But I kept going all out.

On the boat, I could see a few silhouettes. One of these was holding his arms up in the air with his fists tightly clasped. It was Jim Montrella, and that was his signal for "You are doing great." Hans was yelling that I was doing well, but I had no idea if this meant eight or nine hours.

Quickly, I took another peak. The rocks were on my right; I was swimming parallel to the shore. *Why?* We were going to the exact beach where Lynne had landed, so that no one could say that I did not swim as far as she.

With 800 yards left, the dingy was lowered into the water. I wanted to ask Hans what time it was, but felt I could not stop so close to the finish. Instead, I tried to pick it up, one more time.

A second later, I passed a rocky point on my right side. Thinking this was the finish, I quickly took a peek. I hoped to see my family, but no one was there except for a few Boy Scouts on the hill. This thought immediately slipped from my mind as I saw the bottom. It drew closer and closer, until I was able to touch it. I stood up and took three steps beyond the water's edge. I had done it.

In the background I could hear everyone yelling, especially Siga. All I wanted to know was the time. Hans enthusiastically said it was 7:20 a.m. As he hugged me, I began to cry. I had really broken the record, and by so much, too! I had given everything those last three hours.

My body was tingling. The rocks under my feet hurt as I stood there in a daze. Hans quickly wrapped me up in a towel and lifted me into the dinghy. Everybody was still screaming as we were rowed back towards the boat. My official time was seven hours, fifteen minutes, and fifty-five seconds; over an hour and a half under Lynne's record of eight hours thirty-two minutes.

As I was pulled aboard the *Bandido,* Siga, Jim, and everyone there hugged me. I felt so good. We had succeeded. It was a group venture— they had helped me tremendously. I was indebted to them, and we would share this memory the rest of our lives.

Then, all of a sudden, I wondered why I did not see my family. *Where was my family? I had wanted them to be there, but they had missed the finish. Oh my God. What will I do? Where can they be? What will I say? What will my mother say or do?* All these thoughts overwhelmed me. Now I was anxious and worried.

THE AFTER AFFECTS

L imbless, I sat on the edge of the boat, musing. I refused to get dressed. I had to wait for my family. Siga and Syndi enveloped me with towels. Numerous times they tried to convince me to take a shower, but I was not doing anything until I saw my family. I felt badly because they were not there. The swim meant so much to me. I wanted them to be there at the finish, and I knew they did, too. Something must have gone wrong. Worse, I knew my mother would be furious if she missed seeing me finish.

My thoughts turned to all the effort that went into arranging transportation for my family to see the finish. There had been many difficulties. First, were the boat reservations. When I called to make these, I explained to the ticket seller what I was doing. She immediately connected me with Chuck Slocombe, the manager of the Catalina Cruisers, an organization which transports travelers to the Isthmus and Avalon and back three times a day. Confidently, I told him that I needed five tickets so that my family could be at the finish of my Catalina Channel crossing. Furthermore, I declared that I would break the record. Graciously, he offered free round-trip passage for them. I was very surprised at his offer and his belief in me. Next, I made reservations for them to stay at a motel at the Isthmus of Catalina. The final and most difficult arrangement I had to make was for transportation from the motel to the Doctor's Cove, a long, winding, forty-five minute drive or a ten-minute boat ride. Unfortunately, no one could give us a commitment, so we had to find another way. Ultimately, we decided that once my mother arrived on the island she would arrange for a vehicle only if a boat could not be chartered or rented for the short journey.

Another problem was the exact name of the cove where I was to finish. While we were making transportation arrangements, we learned that the cove was called by different names. The navigator called it Doctor's Cove, but in actuality it was Cherry Cove. This created some confusion for everyone.

Besides my family, Gary Troyer, his wife, Jan, and their two sons were also going along for the finish. My mother was able to arrange for the water taxi to take them to the finish point. However, they disagreed over my possible arrival time. My mother felt I would be done at 7:15 a.m. Somehow she knew; she always seemed to know my times ahead of time. No one else agreed with her on this, so she deferred to Gary's opinion because he had been my college coach for the last few years. No one believed I would break the record of eight hours except Mom, so they decided to leave the dock at 7:15 a.m.

As they got into the water taxi, two other men also climbed aboard, thinking it would return them to their boats. Soon, they realized they were in error, and then persuaded the driver to drop them off first. This ten-minute detour would prevent my family and friends from seeing me finish.

My thoughts were interrupted when a small boat approached, started to pass, and then abruptly stopped. Despite being smothered in towels, I waddled over to the side of the boat and saw the faces of my family and friends. The looks on their faces as they gazed up at me were disheartening. They were all so sad. They smiled, but disappointment was written throughout.

As my mother climbed on board the boat, she jokingly asked, "Could you not have swum any faster?" She had wanted to be at the finish, and had been cheated out of it. She did not know what to say or do. I did not know what to say, either. All I wanted was her love and acknowledgment. Quickly, the rest of my family came over and hugged me. The Troyers said hello and disappeared to talk with Siga and Hans. They, and everyone who was on the crossing, stayed out of the way so that I could be with my family.

Tensions were high. My family was very disappointed. For a few moments my mother spoke with me about the race, and then she abruptly asked why Barry and his girlfriend, Kelly, could not have gone on the crossing. Just then, Barry came over and said that he thought that there was so much room on the boat he could have gone and not been in anybody's way. My mind reeled. Prior to the swim, I had asked if my brother could go along on the boat. After much contemplation, Siga said yes, but only Barry could go. Shortly after, I was told that Barry's girlfriend wanted to go with him, but Siga said this was not possible. So, Barry was told there was no room.

I was tired and did not want to deal with this any longer. I wanted to cry or scream out loud. It was just too much! I wish they had been at the finish, but nothing could change that now. Then my mother asked why we had left Doctor's Cove? What if they had gone by car? I could not think of an answer to either of her questions. Finally, with a deep sigh, I told her it was neither the time nor the place to discuss it. With that, my mother walked away very pissed off. I let out a few tears I had been holding until this encounter ended.

Syndi and my sister helped me get dressed. Even though I was exhausted, I wanted to discuss my swim with Siga. So many thoughts and feelings were rushing through my mind. Also, I desired to thank everyone else, which I still had not had a chance to do. Unfortunately, as soon as the boat landed, my family jumped off and waited for me to do the same. So, I said thank you and goodbye to Siga and the crew, and I left with my family.

We strolled up the pier and then rode the bus to the motel. Since I was still very cold, my mother suggested I take a shower and meet them in the dining room. As I entered the room, everyone started clapping. I was embarrassed, but it was a very nice gesture, and it made me feel very good.

While they ate, I drank a cup of hot chocolate, unable to eat. Food was just not very appealing right then. The same feeling had overcome me during the swim. Before the race, my mom and I had baked lots of chocolate chip cookies for me, but during the swim the thought of them seemed repulsive, so I didn't get to enjoy them.

The atmosphere in the dining room was more relaxed than on the boat. Everyone was beginning to loosen up, and I could communicate with them. Sadly, this tranquility was disturbed when the phone began to ring. The first of many reporters was calling, and the questions began. Over and over I had to answer the same question, but the one question which always made me laugh was, "Are you not afraid of sharks?" My typical answer was "Of course, but I do not think about them" or, "That was my coach's problem" or, "Only when I hear the music from *Jaws*!" The latter was printed in *The Los Angeles Times*!

After breakfast, we returned to the Isthmus, since I still needed to call the various people who had supported my crossing. Perhaps I should have had someone else do this, but I did not think of it at the time. The calls took about a half hour which took more time away from my family, but they had to be done.

Exhausted from my long day, I returned to the motel and lay down while everyone else packed. My sister started talking, and gradually the conversation drifted to my swim. Unable to sleep, I joined in, although I found it hard to express my feelings about the swim. My brother came into the room and joined in the conversation. While I talked, they were really interested in what I was saying, and even began to ask questions. Then my mother walked in and said it was time to check out of the motel.

As I rose to go outside, I almost fell over. All of a sudden I felt drained; my body felt like rubber. My mother told me to lie down on the lounge chair in the sun for a while. Every few seconds, I would doze off, unable to stay awake, even though I wanted to talk more with my family. Wrapped in a cocoon of my tiredness and memories of the day, I fell asleep. The sun felt very nice. A little while later, with great effort, I got up. Finally, we left and walked to the Isthmus to wait for the *Catalina Cruiser* to arrive.

Since I was afraid I might get seasick, I took a seasick pill. By the time I got aboard, I could barely keep my eyes open. It was a beautiful, sunny day. The clouds had all disappeared; the water was very blue and mystifying. There was a slight breeze, so we sat on the benches on the deck. I lay down with my head next to my mother's legs and instantly fell asleep.

The crossing took a little over three hours. At one point, the skipper pointed out a school of sharks off the port side. For some unknown reason this announcement woke me. I ventured a quick peek. Not surprising, they were headed for the Catalina Channel. After a few seconds of contemplation and a nervous laugh, I went back to sleep.

As we left the steamer, I went to thank Chuck Slocombe for giving my family free passage, and to tell him how I had done. Chuck wanted some photographs of me with the whole family for the newspapers. After the pictures, my parents had to drive back to Santa Clara because my mother had class in the morning at San Jose State and my father had to be back at work. Barry, Kelly, and I were going to spend a few days at my sister's home in Thousand Oaks, then tour Universal Studios and Magic Mountain before returning home.

It was a long trip to Thousand Oaks as we hit the afternoon rush-hour traffic. I slept until we stopped at a restaurant for dinner. I'd been awake for almost thirty-five hours, not counting a few hours sleep I had on the boat and in the car. I spent the evening watching TV, talking to family and friends on the phone, and speaking with my sister.

As I tried to sleep that night, many thoughts rushed through my head. *Why had I not arranged to have the boat call the motel an hour prior to my finish?* I decided that I had done many stupid things. At the same time I wondered, *Why did I worry about all of this?* Dealing with the feelings of so many people added to the pressures I felt. So many components were involved in a crossing, and some situations seemed to be beyond my control!

The next morning, the three of us, Barry, Kelly, and I, drove to Marineland to see John finish. On the drive to the Mainland, we encountered bumper-to-bumper traffic. This added a half hour to our traveling time.

As it turned out, John had finished ten minutes before we arrived. Luckily, we met his family and followed them to the Twenty-Second Street landing in San Pedro. John had broken the men's record by ten seconds. He had swum eight hours forty-nine minutes and fifty seconds, according to the three official timers. Dave Cox had been eighteen when he set the record; however, John was only fifteen years old. It was a great swim.

When I reached the landing, I was astonished. Three major TV channels had sent crews to cover the swim. Furthermore, about thirty friends were on hand. This was so different from the finish of my swim the day before. The publicity for my swim had been rather disorganized. As it turned out, I needed someone to coordinate all the news. This was another facet involved with such a swim that I needed to learn.

Unfortunately, I received some criticisms for the direction I swam; it was considered swimming the easy way. That really surprised and hurt me. I had swum from the mainland to Catalina because I wanted to break the record for the fastest overall swim, regardless of the direction or whether a man or woman had set it. It just happened to be held by another woman. John, however, had swum the other way to do just that. Prior to the swim, he had no illusion to break the men's record. He just wanted to make it. The fact that he set the record was added glory.

After leaving the finish of John's swim, the three of us, Barry, Kelly, and I, spent the rest of the day relaxing. We went to Universal Studios, and then took an excursion to Magic Mountain prior to returning to Northern California.

I now had a lot of free time to contemplate the swim and my future. The only question was, "What would I do next?" Prior to the swim, I had spoken with Siga about doing a double crossing. Because of the mix up at the finish, I thought I would swim from the mainland and back, and, hopefully, avoid any hassles. This would prevent a recurrence of the problems I encountered with the first swim, and my family would be there to share the joy with me. Also, there was a hotel at the start and the finish. However, there was still the possibility of incurring criticism for not going the same way as Greta Andersen had in 1958. She swam from the Island to the mainland in ten hours forty-nine minutes, rested twenty-nine minutes, and returned. Greta's swim took twenty-six hours fifty minutes. I did not want people to say I took the easy way again. Similarly, I contemplated the latter direction in order to break the one-way record and to break my own on the return. That would be a feat in itself!

The swim was over. It was probably the greatest thing in my life up to that point, and all I felt was guilty, upset, frustrated, and unsure of how to deal with my family and especially my mother and her hurt feelings.

But what could I say to appease my family now? I was sorry, but did they understand what I went through? How I felt? I wanted them to be a part of my swimming, but I also hoped that they would appreciate and be proud of what I did and why. They did, but they were disappointed they were not a part of it. So, fixing the problems that prevented my family from sharing in my joy made the most sense to me. I knew what to fix for the double crossing—I could *Just Try One More* to get it right!

THE FINAL YEAR AT
POMONA COLLEGE

I returned to Pomona in the fall of 1976 for my final year at college, my last collegiate season. I also had many plans for the future. First, there was law school. I applied to six schools, each in California. The only difficulty I saw was swimming. If I began law school, that would be the end of my swimming. I did not know if I would be ready to quit in a year, after swimming for almost twenty-one years.

Second, I had my ROTC summer camp obligation. I would have to fulfill it in 1977, try to arrange another deferment, or leave the program. Again, that would also mean no swimming because I would be gone all summer. With the completion of camp, I would become a Second Lieutenant in the Army, with a two-year active duty and a four-year reserve duty obligation or a six-year reserve obligation ahead of me.

I joined ROTC in the middle of my sophomore year because an awesome military history class, 1945 to 1970s, had inspired me. My junior year a military law class was offered. As I planned on attending law school, this was a great fit, but I was told the scholarship I earned could not be used for law school. Because I had been misled, I was allowed to leave ROTC at the beginning of my senior year.

Third, I applied for a Watson Graduate Fellowship. This fellowship allowed the recipient to spend a year studying something she was interested in, without limitations or obligations. It was a long shot, but it was worth a try. My proposal was to study swimming throughout Europe and ultimately swim the English Channel, also known as the Channel. Jim Montrella, of LAC, gave me the names of coaches throughout Europe. I wrote to each about my potential study, asking if it was possible to train and stay with them or a family. Thirteen coaches responded immediately and positively.

Lastly, I considered looking for a coaching job. I really enjoyed coaching, but I did not know if it could be a lifetime career. So many options, so many decisions, all of which I had to make or had to be made for me.

As for collegiate swimming, my goal was to do very well at the Collegiate Nationals. Finally, the 1650 free and the 400 individual medley had been added to my planned roster of future swims. Furthermore, there was even a possibility of a small Collegiate Nationals, Division III. As for our team, Pomona had a good crop of freshmen women. I would not have to go to the Nationals by myself, and above all, we would send a relay or two.

With regards to my ocean swimming, there were four possibilities: swimming the English Channel, a double of Catalina, the professional circuit in Canada, or the proposed $25,000 race across the Catalina Channel. The latter was the most impressive. In the first weeks of October, I had two meetings with Jim and Siga to discuss my future. They could not believe all the irons I had in the fire, but they were most concerned with my swimming goals. They felt I had a long and prosperous marathon career in front of me and they did not want to see it slip away. Regardless of the three swimming options for the next summer, they suggested I attempt to settle the ROTC camp problem as soon as possible, and let everything else fall into place.

The next question they had was the amount of LAC workouts I would be able to attend throughout the year. I was skeptical about being able to do much. Through March, I would be able to attend LAC workouts on weekends if I had time. After the collegiate season ended, however, I would be spending considerably less time in the water since I had three four-hour comprehensive history examinations in April and May. If I did not pass them, I would not graduate. Jim told me not to worry, and then changed the subject. My academics were clearly up to me!

Jim had figured out my maximum mileage and the average for the past summer. The average was 20,000 meters a day, while the maximum was 27,000 meters. Jim was impressed, as not too many swimmers in the world were doing that much. While he had been at the 1976 Olympics, he had heard of a few Russians who had swum 30,000 meters. Curiously, he asked if I could do that. Without blinking an eye, I said, "Sure." I had gone 27,000 yards in the pool at college, and more in the ocean. Then Jim asked if I could swim 36,000 meters straight in the pool. Again, I confidently said yes, but I was wondering what he was leading up to. (I found this out before I really had time to think about it.) "When?" was his final question.

When? . . . He suggested I attempt it before the end of the year. A little startled, I agreed to do it over the Christmas vacation. That would give me time to recover, get back in shape, and give Jim time to forget about it. With this I left, and did not return for over a month.

Besides schoolwork, I had a few reasons for not making the ocean workouts. I was struggling over the early-season workouts. For me there was no consistency, and each time I attended, I caught a cold. Another thing that troubled me was the other swimmers. None of them had the long commute or the commitments I had to restrict their training, and yet I felt that each workout I attended I had to prove to them that I was still number one. I sprinted at everything; I had to be first. I enjoyed doing this, pushing myself, but it was still very frustrating because I saw how well they were doing.

The final thing that kept me away from the ocean was that I felt that I no longer belonged there. Everyone was very nice and always happy to see me, but I was never comfortable while there. The close relationship we had during the summer was gone. Our club was larger, as a few swimmers from LAC had joined. I really liked them and was glad they had joined, but there was a difference; the group dynamics had changed. One of the people I always looked forward to seeing was

Syndi, but she was involved in many other things, and was unable to attend most of the workouts. As it turned out, she missed the few I attended or had to rush off at other times before we could talk. We never had time to talk now, and I missed that.

In addition, I now had problems communicating with Siga. Every time I tried to talk with her, she seemed to drift away. I did not say anything; I did not tell her I was having problems. Unlike the year before, I never asked to stay at her house; I just did not want to intrude. It was too hard with all of my feelings for her. I was going through personal changes. I was training with a great college team, and I had tons of studying to do. Instead of communicating my feelings and problems to Siga, I just stayed away. My senior year in college was very challenging, and I felt it was too important to stay focused on my studies.

In October, there was a marathon swimming meeting. Chuck Lidell, from Catalina, wanted to discuss the proposed $25,000 race. He was interested in holding this race since it was the 50th anniversary of the 1927 swim. Unfortunately, Chuck realized that he did not have the time, desire, or knowledge to plan or organize such an endeavor. The swim was canceled even before it reached the planning stages. That was the end of my chances of $25,000, and my money for law school.

Despite his misgivings, Chuck planned a memorial at Catalina for January 15, 1977, exactly fifty years after the swim. He invited not only the few living participants in the 1927 swim, but every successful Catalina Channel swimmer since that time. I was told of this event just prior to my Christmas vacation. I had arranged to train with LAC from December 17 until the 23. Also, I had planned to swim the 36,000 meters on the 23rd, and then fly home later that evening to spend Christmas with my family. Then the following week I would train with the Santa Clara Swim Club under the careful guidance of Olympian Mitch Ivey.

Thursday, December 23, I had to get up fairly early to prepare for the 36,000 meter swim. I was not too hungry, so I only had some juice and a Breakfast Jack from Jack-in-the-Box on the way to the pool. The swim was scheduled to begin at seven. Hopefully, I would be finished by four o'clock.

During the first two hours, Siga's group was in the pool while the seniors were exercising. Then the novice team had the pool. At 11:00 a.m. the senior group reentered the water. It was interesting to watch the various people swimming and the others on deck, but with all the swimmers in the pool, the water was unusually choppy. At one o'clock everything settled down. The seniors did not finish until three o'clock. At last the pool was peaceful and empty, but lonely. With the passing hours, my pace slowed down. At the beginning I had been holding 1:20 per hundred, but by the early afternoon, I was struggling to maintain 1:26s and 1:27s. My back ached, as did my knee. With each flip turn a sharp pain went up my back. Gradually I dropped to 1:28s. Four thousand, 3000, 2000 to go. Then the senior group was back in the water. I tried to pick up my pace; each length seemed longer than the one before, 1500, 1000, 500. As I flipped with only 400 meters to go, Jim had the seniors line up along the length of the pool. As I passed each swimmer, he would yell encouragements. Some went underwater and made faces. I was sprinting each length, as hard as I could. Thinking I was done, I stopped, only to be told that I had two more lengths. I had just sprinted a 1:14 and now I had a hundred more. Exhausted, I burst the last hundred in 1:12. As I finished, everyone started cheering; I had made it. My eyes were swollen; my arms, my head, and body ached. I was numb and dizzy, but I did not care; I was finished. Twenty-four miles completed, and in a decent time.

During the swim, I stopped only three times, at 12,000 meters, 24,000 meters, and 30,000 meters. Quickly, I swallowed a few ounces of ERG and pushed off again. Surprisingly, I was done at 3:30 p.m. For eight hours thirty-two minutes, I swam back and forth, mesmerized by the black line on the bottom of the pool. At times, the swim was boring, exciting, exhausting. A rotation of swimmers counted the lengths.

As I climbed out of the pool, a reporter stopped me and asked me how I felt. He also wanted to know when I would do it again. I just laughed, and did not make any commitments or comments.

As planned, I flew home that evening, enjoyed two days off, and then began a hard week of training with the Santa Clara Swim Club before returning to Pomona College.

TO BEGIN AGAIN

My final collegiate season was the best pool season ever, despite having a problem with my balance system. At the Nationals, I was third in the 400 IM, 500, and 1650 free, fourth in the 200 free, sixth in the 200 IM, and was tenth in our 800 free relay. Each was a lifetime swim.

When I returned home from Nationals, I found two letters accepting me at my first two choices of law school, Southwestern, and University of San Francisco. As I was deciding which school to attend, I received a letter from the Watson Foundation. I was a recipient of the Watson Graduate Fellowship. I was ecstatic, as this meant one year in Europe and my chance at the English Channel.

For my spring break, ROTC'er boyfriend, Brad, invited me to spend the week with him in Georgia. As the balance problem had cleared up, I was able to swim in the Atlantic Ocean. Then, that night Brad and I went to see the movie, *Rocky*, which had just come out in the theaters that week. I was so excited. It was an inspirational movie. Once back at his place, my boyfriend thought I would finally want to have sex with him. He knew I didn't believe in premarital sex. I had been raped once before in Germany, which he also knew. These did not seem to matter to him, and in that spring, 1977, I was raped by my boyfriend.

Two of my ribs were cracked, and I had trouble breathing. I went to the hospital by ambulance. Sadly, I was too embarrassed to tell the ER doctor what had happened (it was the seventies). I flew home the next day. I was very depressed. I told my parents I fell out of a tree. I was unable to swim again until mid-May because of the broken ribs, but with comprehensives, finals, and graduation, I postponed my reentry into the ocean until the beginning of June.

Not until early June, did I meet with Jim and Siga about my summer swim plans. Jim said anyone can set one world record, but few set two. This intrigued me and led to my decision to swim the double crossing of the Catalina Channel. I wanted the record, but the work involved seemed insurmountable. At that point I did not have the desire, either mentally or physically, but it would come in time . . . I thought.

I had arranged to spend the summer in Redondo Beach with Cindy Cleveland, her mother, and grandmother. I moved in on the evening of my college graduation. Since my parents had split up by then, besides my ocean teammates, only my mother, sister and her husband were coming to my graduation. After an exciting ceremony, we left for a quiet celebration dinner with my family and ocean teammates. Unfortunately, my father showed up, and my mother was not pleased. She started screaming, refused to have dinner with me, and then left me standing all alone on the sidewalk in front of a restaurant. Fortunately, my ocean teammates showed up shortly thereafter. We enjoyed a celebratory dinner and then we had a cake later that night.

The following morning my summer training began, and that meant a new challenge. My training began on a rather shaky foundation and consequently, I felt I never achieved the level of performance I was capable of nor was my attitude 100 percent during this period. I never completely overcame my initial doubts. I wanted the swim, the records, but sometimes I did not want the work. I worked hard and steadily throughout the summer but rarely did I put out that little extra that had made me so successful in the past. I lacked a certain feeling more than anything, and this affected my psychological preparation. That made the difference between a good and a bad performance, an excellent or great performance. My hang-up was that I was never satisfied with a good performance, only a great one. I was pushing myself too hard, expecting too much.

As in the past, Jim and Siga worked together to coordinate my pool and ocean training. The first week of the summer, I began very gradually, swimming only two workouts a day, one in the pool and then short ocean training. The latter was very difficult. At first I was really scared, especially when I had to work out by myself. The others had not finished school, so our ocean team training had not begun daily workouts. Seeing the fish, adjusting to the water temperature, dealing with the waves, and regaining the confidence to swim hundreds of yards offshore took awhile to reacquire.

Being out of condition further frustrated me. I did not like swimming poorly; I wanted to be back in shape immediately. My times in the ocean and the pool were deplorable, although expected. Jim and Siga constantly reminded me to swim through everything for the first week, and to stay positive, as it would take a while to get in shape again.

I had to build up slowly, otherwise I could get sick, overexert, or possibly damage my muscles. Numerous times I told myself, *Just keep going, the times are insignificant. It will get harder before it gets easier, but your coaches, friends and family are behind you.*

I was very impatient. I wanted to go 100 percent from the first day, not missing a workout. I did not like sleeping in or missing a pool workout, afraid I wouldn't get back into a routine. Further, I had too much time to think, to think about what life had to offer and with this, my doubts emerged. *Would it be worth it?* From a psychological standpoint, the gradual buildup had a negative effect. I felt stifled. I was unable to rechannel or revitalize my initial enthusiasm.

On the other hand, my living situation more than made up for the emptiness I was feeling, and for my dissatisfaction with my swimming. Grandma Cleveland, at ninety years old, told many fascinating stories and often kept me in stitches for hours. Her antics, playing with Cindy's dog or her relationship with a would be "boyfriend," kept everyone else on their toes. When I moved in, her health was a concern, and as the summer drifted on, it progressively deteriorated. Nevertheless, she always seemed to be happy when someone called or stopped in for a visit. In mid-August her health took a turn for the worse, so I moved in with the Yorks, so there would be more room for her relatives.

Cindy's mother and I had spent many evenings in in-depth discussions on a variety of subjects. Emotionally, I was alienated from my swimming, and rebelled against others around me. I was going through a period in my life in which I did not want to give anyone credit for helping me. I felt as if I was doing most things by myself, but everyone else wanted credit for it. It was nice to have someone to talk with especially after spending hours alone in the water.

As for the workouts, they were scheduled for six days a week; only Sunday was free. The only races my teammates and I were required to attend was the Seal Beach 10-Mile and the Catalina Classic 15 miler. Siga preferred we rest on Sunday rather than swim the other shorter races; however, the final choice was always our own. At the beginning of the summer I decided that I would not swim any other races. I knew I both wanted and needed a day off, away from the water. Otherwise, I felt saturated and it was hard to motivate myself during the tedious training of the week. I needed time to recuperate; to write letters, to visit friends, to have a good time, or to do nothing (this was, of course, decades before PCs).

Within the first three weeks of training I improved significantly, but something wasn't right about my training. My times were still not as fast as they were the summer before. The long layoff was the rationalization, but I wasn't sure this was the reason. One difference which was very evident was my daydreaming. I seemed to be dreaming throughout the workouts, not really concentrating on what I was doing. It was not until my first nine-mile swim from Hermosa to El Segundo and back on June 23, when I was really pleased with a workout. It was a memorable workout because it was the first time I took off on my own. I felt powerful again, so I sprinted ahead of the others. As much as I was unsure of the course that lay ahead, the sheer exultation of being alone, sprinting as hard as I could, overshadowed any immediate fears I had. I even sprinted through the pier without pausing for long to watch for dangling fishing lines or strong waves which might push me into the pilings. For me, this was a major accomplishment, as I had always been afraid of swimming through the piers. The immense pain I encountered was wonderful; I had my fight back.

Just after the halfway point, Siga began walking along with me. This uplifted me even more. Ten minutes later, however, I briefly lost my confidence when I noticed a dark shadow beneath me. After a few frightful seconds, I realized it was a four-foot shark. Initially, I could not catch my breath. At that point I was passing a barren beach. John and Mary Beth were about five minutes behind me. I was over 150 yards from the shore. The only one around was Siga. Never did that woman in those dark blue shorts, bikini top, with her loosely-tied, long brown hair tucked under a chef's-style white cap, seem more reassuring! Immediately, a calmness came over me. I had nothing to worry about. If the shark was stupid enough to attack me, at least Siga would watch me die. Whenever such thoughts entered my mind, I reacted in the same way: I sprinted until I couldn't sprint any longer. Siga, seeing me take off quickly, attempting to maintain the pace, began signaling me to keep going. She liked it. If she only knew what had inspired me to pick up my pace so drastically! For almost two miles I sprinted, with my eyes closed, of course. Finally, the cold water and my lack of endurance took its toll, and my pace gradually slowed. With great difficulty, I finished. But I finished. I had had an excellent training, and I was very pleased to know I still had my fight.

After the workout I spoke to Siga about her coming to England for my English Channel crossing in 1978. I wanted to give her plenty of time to think about it, and to, hopefully, make a positive decision. She was interested, but it would depend on what she and Hans were doing.

Gradually, my ocean training improved; however, there were times when I just did not have any desire to train. Early one day, after practice, I spoke to Siga about my problems. Siga told me I was still on a trial basis, but I had to make up my mind by mid-July. Also, that I could not allow outside factors to affect my training. Unfortunately, I had no other time to deal with them. I was in the water all day long and needed the rest of the time to get the proper amount of sleep. I had no free time to think. Any spare time I had was spent on errands. I felt as if I were a machine. I was told when to sleep, when to eat, when to swim, and there was nothing else. My mind felt like a vacuum. Nevertheless, I agreed to try to concentrate only on the workout at hand. For a while I was reassured, and this produced rapid improvements in both my pool and ocean workouts. Still, however, I had days of training when I could not concentrate or swim well. Sometimes I just did not feel right. There were days when I could not overcome the struggle, when Siga's proddings were useless, when I just needed time off. Fortunately, with Siga's assistance I was able to persevere and overcome these hardships and continue working.

At times the pressures and anxieties of the training were overwhelming. Each of us had our own way of lightening the situation. My favorite release was to buy a crazy gift or play a harmless practical joke. Too, there were many other ways to make the workout seem less like work and more challenging. Whether this meant racing the others or seeing how far one could get, doing tower sprints against each other, each of us tried them. Siga could also become an entertainer. Each mile of each workout had to be different. They had to be special or it was boring or too taxing mentally. She tried everything to maintain our interests, to help us continually work harder and further, surpassing our former limitations.

One of our favorite releases was Siga's weekly get-togethers at Swenson's Ice Cream parlor after a workout. Besides discussing our training for upcoming swims, we ate a lot of ice cream. On one particular occasion, Tuesday, August 9, 1977, we decided to meet again in ten years—at the same restaurant. A dollar bill was torn into seven pieces—one for each of us: Siga, Syndi, Dan, Cindy, John, Mary Beth, and me. On each one we wrote the time, place, and date of our proposed reunion. After this, each of us contemplated what everyone else would be doing or have done by then. We all agreed that it would be interesting to see what had happened in those ten years. Would the ice cream parlor still be there, and if we put the dollar together, would it still pay for a cup of coffee?

During this time, a few of us usually spent our day off together. Whether we had a barbecue, went to a movie or dinner, or even spent the day at the beach, either body surfing or basking in the sun, we had a good time. Further, at every possible opportunity, although there were not many, we had a party; most of them at the York's home. All of these get-togethers helped to bring us a little closer together and to make the weeks pass quicker.

**Party at the Yorks' home; standing left
to right—Dottie, Betsy, Siga**

THE TESTS

The two important races of the summer, the Seal Beach 10-Mile and the Isthmus to Avalon 15 Mile were rapidly approaching. The Seal Beach race was expected to be very interesting since John Sorige, star distance swimmer of BYU and a team member of LAC was planning to swim. For two weeks, he confidently told me how easily he would win.

The Tuesday prior to the Seal Beach swim, a few of us had to swim a sixteen-mile workout, the most we had attempted thus far in a single training. I, unfortunately, had to swim two of these workouts in a row. Instead of just the scheduled twelve miles on Wednesday, I had to swim an extra four miles. The last four miles were make-up. We had a challenging, but worthwhile rule, that if you missed training, unless you were deadly ill or excused by Siga, you had to make up the mileage and as soon as possible. At times I owed a lot. During the previous week I had to stay out of the water one day because I had a swollen eye, but Siga insisted that I would have to make up the ten miles and at her convenience. Once Jim found out, he prodded me daily to make up the miles before another week went by. For three days after workout was officially over I did extra miles, but this rapid increase in mileage had detrimental effects. By Thursday, three days before the race at Seal

Beach, I could not move my left shoulder. I could not raise my arm without encountering excruciating pain; I had overworked it. So, I took the day off knowing that I would have to make up that later, too, and immediately began administering a treatment of alternating hot and cold packs on my left shoulder. I continued that for two days, and by Friday afternoon, it seemed a little better. I swam a shorter workout, only nine miles, but without any pressure or speed. Similarly, I swam a mere seven miles on Saturday. The others swam twelve and eight respectively. At this point I was seventeen miles in debt. It was becoming a topic of conversation, and it was beginning to drive me crazy.

Siga almost refused to let me participate in the Seal Beach race because of my shoulder problem. On Saturday, after three phone calls in which I lied about the pain I was having, she finally agreed to let me swim. She had one condition, however, that if I hurt, I had to stop and I was not to use the shoulder as the reason. We both knew I would never quit no matter how much it hurt, and regardless of the outcome, I would not use the shoulder as an excuse. If I swam, I would do my best, and that was all I wanted to do. So, I agreed completely, and reluctantly, she gave her permission.

None of that mattered, however, when I got up at 4:15 a.m. on Sunday, July 24, for the 10 mile race. It was an overcast morning and rather cold. I arrived at the beach by 5:30 a.m. The waves near the Huntington Beach pier were always treacherous and difficult to adapt to, but today the water was very active. Since I had to become accustomed to the vicious swells, I needed a thorough warm-up. Furthermore, it usually took me two or three miles to feel comfortable and to build up my pace. Prior to a race, however, I never swam for more than a half mile. Instead, I would use the first mile or so of the race as warm-up. But on this occasion, I was not thinking clearly. Because of my shoulder pain, I needed an even longer warm-up, but I still could not adjust to the pain. In addition, the currents were stronger than I had expected, and I was nervous. Whether it was the excitement or the pain I was feeling, I remained in the water only a few minutes. Still, I did not loosen up very well at all. At the same time, I was afraid of overdoing it. This error in judgment of not warming up enough, would become a detriment to me in the race; a mental error.

The swimmers lined up diagonally on the beach beyond the water. The final preparations complete, Mr. Yeo began to give the starting command when someone started running too soon, causing a false start. Everyone was called back, and we lined up once again. The air was filled with excitement as twenty swimmers anxiously awaited the gunshot. Numerous friends and parents stood just beyond the swimmers nervously awaiting the beginning and pondering the outcome. The tension was mounting in all of us!

Bang! We were off running, laughing, jumping, dolphining, and diving through the onslaught of the waves. It took a lot of energy to rapidly swim a few strokes, take a breath, and dive under an overpowering wave. Considering the rapidity and irregularity of the wave sets we were encountering, I assumed it would take almost five minutes of this type of maneuvering before I reached the calm water beyond the surf line. Therefore, I began rather cautiously, not wanting to overdo it at the start. I watched as the others rushed on ahead, but it did not bother me, or so I kept telling myself, although I felt empty and uninspired. Anyway, I just did not feel like expending energy at that point.

Something was occurring that I had not expected, however. In previous years we had to swim straight out, parallel with the pier, circle the buoy, then swim parallel to the coast in a northerly direction for ten (actually eight and a half) miles. There was no buoy, but all the paddlers had stationed themselves as if there was one. Not thinking, I ran directly out, and swam in that direction. I soon realized, however, that several other participants were swimming in an angle away from the pier, with no specific intention of meeting the paddlers. Quickly, I realized that it was not required nor had it been discussed. In those precious minutes, many valuable yards had been lost. After five minutes of conservative swimming and diving, I reached the calm water and discovered I was third, and by a considerable distance; I had conserved too much. John Sorige was in the lead with John York in the second position. My left arm felt like lead; I tried to pick it up, but to no avail.

Gradually, I overcame my physical and mental handicaps, passed John York, and began to gain on John Sorige. By the time I reached the five-mile mark, I was moving fairly well. Hans kept telling me I was gaining on Sorige, but that he had an overwhelming lead. Fortunately, my rhythmic stroke was becoming faster and more powerful with each passing minute. As I reached the jetty, I had no idea how far ahead Sorige was, but Hans could see him. He felt I could catch him. I was not as optimistic, but I pressed on. I could not see anything. As I neared the Seal Beach pier, I attempted to circumvent it and became entangled in various fishing lines. As soon as I broke through them, I looked towards the beach. To my utter amazement, Sorige was less than twenty-five yards in front of me! I was so close. I gave everything I had left, but it was not enough, and I lost to him by seven seconds. Seven seconds in the eight and a half mile swim! If I had another 200 yards I would have caught him, but it did not matter. It was an excellent swim and I was happy.

My time was three hours, exactly. I went to congratulate Sorige and found him utterly exhausted, asleep on the sand. I felt fine and later even swam the one-mile race. He told me later to keep at marathon swimming, but he no longer wanted any part of it.

The following Tuesday I had to swim a seventeen-mile workout. The water was cold and I had motivational problems. At five miles I turned with Mary Beth as I needed some company and a push. We swam together for four miles; then I turned with John. Unfortunately, at this point, Siga arrived. She was very mad when she watched me do this. At ten miles I realized I was wasting my time, so I got out. As I was leaving the water, Siga came up. She calmly asked me what I was doing, but her expression told me that she was very upset. She thought it was unfair of me to turn with John and then leave. She said it would affect him also. Then she stated flatly that I could not leave a workout. Once I began, I had to finish unless the conditions made it impossible to do so. Without responding, I returned to the water. For the first few minutes I was angry, but gradually my speed increased. By the seventeenth mile I was swimming very well. After I finished, I wanted to speak with Siga; however, there were too many other people around. Quietly I dressed and prepared to leave. Siga asked if I wanted my times; I said no. Then she asked if I was coming the next day. I simply answered that I did not know. Of course I was coming; what a silly question. I was just being sullen.

The next few days the fog came in rather heavily, making it impossible to continue on our own. For safety reasons, we swam in a group as close to shore as possible. Swimming in a group has its positive and negative aspects. For the latter, it is hard for the faster swimmer to swim at a slower pace so the others can remain abreast since this makes one very cold. On the other hand, it is more fun as there are more races, playing around, and more communication than normal. One morning as we turned at the jetty, we contemplated sneaking off to a nearby 31 Flavors ice cream parlor and then returning in an hour or so, as the dense fog would have hidden us from Siga. She would never have known, as she would have been too busy running up and down the beach looking for us! Of course we never did this to her.

At dusk on Friday, July 24, our group, with the accompaniment of seven paddlers and four officials, sailed to Catalina. It was a romantic cruise with a full moon and light breeze. One by one the sleeping bags were spread out on the deck. The mystique of the evening enraptured me, but I was unable to sleep; I just dreamed. Once the vessel rippled to a stop in the outskirts of the Isthmus, I drifted into a brief but peaceful sleep.

We were awakened early the next morning as everything had to be packed and properly stowed. As soon as breakfast was completed the swimmers were taken ashore. I had decided to drink ERG every hour as I wanted to do on my double crossing. My stroke never felt good. I had a bad day and finished second. Hans also had a bad day. Siga had to take over paddling. I could smell the perfume she was wearing. This made me feel better, but the pain in my shoulder was unbelievable. It was a disappointing day except for Siga paddling.

After a day off, I arrived on Monday with a smile on my face despite the fact that I was the only one going twenty miles. The beach was deserted. The sand was still cold, the birds were in flight. In the east the first flickers of sunlight could be seen. My training was excellent, between twenty and twenty-two minutes a mile in the afternoon chop. A chop is water that bounces one to two feet, and on a bad day will go three or more feet! It makes it difficult to keep up your pace and breathe while you're fighting the chop. The workout took seven hours, fifty-five minutes even with two breaks at ten and fifteen miles. At the latter, I commented to Siga that there were only thirty days left before the swim. Furthermore, I had reevaluated my training and I realized that I had to give more—110 percent. Although there was no such thing, I had to find 110 percent.

The rest of the week, my spirits were high and this was reflected in my workouts. That Friday my mother arrived. We had a relaxing weekend, with many long walks, a few evenings out with Mrs. Cleveland, and a cookie-baking session, but accomplished some business, too. Siga discussed the arrangements of my upcoming crossing. As for the English Channel, she agreed to send workouts to my mother during the year, but she still was undecided as to whether or not she would be going. She wanted to, but other obligations might prevent her. As quickly as the weekend approached, it drifted away. At 4:50 a.m. on Sunday, I rose for a workout. Shortly thereafter, I bid farewell to my mother, knowing I would not see her again until the night before the crossing. In the eerie silence, as we parted, a sense of loneliness, of being a drifter, crept over me.

After saying goodbye, I went to an early workout. Once in the water, I felt weak and slow during the workout that day. The water was extremely choppy, and I began to experience extreme pain in my left shoulder, even though I was getting stronger. I caught a second wind, and completed the workout by sprinting two twenty-minute miles despite the choppy sea. The swim was very encouraging.

On Monday, August 15, I was plagued with problems again. It was a miserable day. The water was cold, around 63°. Slowly I made my way through the waves. I was tired and cold. I could not swim anymore. As I stood up in the surf line, I saw Siga standing in front of me with my ice chest. She was smiling as usual. I pretended not to see her. Beyond her I could see John getting dressed. I wondered why he had gotten out. I still had ten miles to do; I had already gone twenty miles.

As I approached Siga, I told her I did not want to swim anymore. I could not look directly at her; instead, I glanced across the forlorn beach. I had quit too many workouts already. Meekly I turned and gazed at the dark water. It was so frustrating. During the last few miles the ocean had become very rough.

For a few seconds an eerie silence engulfed us. I started shivering. My legs were numb and my back ached with pain. Finally, Siga said we had already discussed this workout. I had decided to go thirty miles when she felt twenty-five was sufficient. She reminded me that I had thought it was necessary for my mental preparation. Furthermore, I had agreed that once I had begun, I could not quit. Since the conditions were not very good, however, she said if I went only twenty-five miles, she would be pleased. Siga was so patient. I couldn't believe it, but I wasn't strong again that day. I shook my head. "No, I cannot; I cannot make it." Siga abruptly turned to me and asked if I would quit during my crossing. Thoroughly expecting a "no" answer, she was shocked when I blurted out, "Yes, if the water is this cold, I would stop. It is not worth it." I stated this in a matter-of-fact way, not thinking about what I was saying. Further, I did not look at her when I said it. I couldn't.

Siga was infuriated. She told me to shut up, that it was worth it, that I could not stop; I had gone through too much. Besides, she pointed out, I only had three more weeks to go and then I would be done. If I did not want to swim anymore, that was my choice. However, I would be wasting my talent. Finally, she said, "Do not quit now, and **just try one more** at a time."

Still I did not answer. Slowly, tears started running down my face. I wanted to get out, but I seemed to be frozen in position. My mind drifted from one thought to another. I did not move; I did not speak. My head was pounding. *I must be going insane. What am I doing here? No, come on, you have to keep going. Come on relax.*

At this point Siga changed her approach. She reached down and pulled out a bottle of ERG and some cookies. Then she asked me how much I wanted to drink. I started crying and turned to her. We hugged each other and cried and laughed together. She agreed to get in to paddle with me for the next five miles. I swam five more miles, one mile at a time, with Siga at my side. I made it through another workout with her guidance and support.

Sometimes it was so hard. The water, the conditions, the weather, they always changed. One day it would be cold and overcast, the next, sunny, then rainy and stormy. Regardless, we had to train. Also, I trained for five hours a day for pool competition and six to eight hours for the single crossing, and I got used to those schedules. Now, the nine to thirteen hours a day for this swim seemed physically and mentally impossible at times. Fortunately, Siga helped me achieve each and every workout. Three things kept me going: first, the desire to become the fastest channel swimmer in the world; second, my mother; and third, my coach, Siga Gudmudson Albrecht.

Unlike most sports, the coach is an integral component of marathon swimming. Not only does this person have to write and run the workouts, but further must continually reassure and support the swimmer. The swimmer needs to have full faith in her coach. For this relationship to succeed, the coach must know every facet of the swimmer, her likes, dislikes, her feelings, her very essence. It is a twenty-four-hour job. It is rare to find someone who is that dedicated to another, willing to give herself totally to the success of another.

My teammates and I were lucky to have Siga. Day after day, hour after hour, she was on the beach taking our times, counting our strokes, correcting our strokes, working on our mental attitudes, and discussing our upcoming swim arrangements. Each day brought a new problem. Whether it was the conditions or our mental attitudes, she had to get us through. If she had to deal with only one swimmer, her job would have been difficult, but she had seven of us: seven swimmers with different goals, attitudes, and moods.

Marathon swimming is a difficult sport, ever-changing and always challenging. The mental attitude can make or break an athlete. That is why a good coach is a necessity. To become a world-class marathon swimmer one needs hours of fast training a day, total dedication to a goal, a good coach, money to pay for the swims, and luck. Because in the end, if everything else is perfect and the conditions are not, there will be problems. But that, is, marathon swimming.

Within two days, the weather changed abruptly. By Wednesday we found ourselves alone on the beach in the middle of a torrential rainstorm. It was very strange. The scheduled workout was ten miles. Never having been particularly fond of training in the rain, I swam quickly with the intention of finishing as soon as possible. I breezed through two miles and was way ahead of the others when I began to run into a stream of garbage. I was swimming into children's toys, old plastic balls, mashed fruits, sticks, logs, and other debris which were floating in the water. The smell was ghastly. Half the beach was covered with the rubber junk. With each stroke, more and more junk covered the water. The sewers overflowed and this was being washed into the ocean via the Seal Beach waterway. I lifted my head and tried to get around it, but that was not possible. The workout had to continue despite the disgusting conditions. It was so disgusting I decided to get out. I was covered with trash. Siga was furious! However, once I left she moved the other swimmers to the other side of the pier.

Two days later, I spoke with Dottie York about the recent swimming conditions. Dottie hosted most of our parties and BBQs and was a second mother to all of us. She supported Siga and yet was a friend to each of us. If we ever needed anything she would take care of it. As I sat in her car talking about the conditions, she just listened. After talking to Dottie, I went back to the beach and made up the mileage. I was very lucky to live in her home for a month, and to be able to spend time with all of the Yorks, especially John.

THE DOUBLE CROSSING

A fter a long summer of training, my Catalina crossing date was rapidly approaching. The Monday before the swim, August 29, I began the protein—carbohydrate diet. This consisted of three days of overloading proteins, then three days of carbohydrates. The theory is that in the first three days your body is depleted of carbohydrates and is begging for them. Thus, once the second half of the diet begins, the body hoards the carbohydrates by storing them, fearing that the supply may be cut off at any time. Thus, for a race, especially a long-distance race, there is more energy available.

The first day of the diet I had a fourteen-mile workout. The only things I could eat at the beach were pieces of meat and cheese, while at the same time John was eating cookies and drinking ERG. Somehow I made it through the first day fairly well without too much temptation. The second day was a little harder, especially with John eating two bowls of mint chocolate chip ice cream and three chocolate eggs right in front of me. I wanted to cheat so much, but I did not. At workout that morning, Siga asked if I would like to come to her house the next morning after practice. She knew I was getting a little jittery, so she invited me to her house a few days earlier than expected. So, after workout on Wednesday, I moved in. That also happened to be the last day of the protein portion of the diet.

On Wednesday evening Hans convinced me to try a protein drink that he and a friend had developed especially for the doubles. Siga had warned me that it looked disgusting and did not taste much better, but said that it was very beneficial. Besides, Hans had spent a lot of time creating it. I was not into protein drinks or food. Nevertheless, I agreed to give it a try, but only for Hans. I did not want to hurt his feelings. When he entered the room with a large mug filled with a thick, darkish, milky-looking substance, I wanted to run. (Something I don't do well.) Besides the drink, which consisted of fertile eggs, lectin, bee honey, and numerous other goodies, Hans presented me with a handful of pills. There were forty in all, ten alfalfa, ten kelp, fifteen beef liver, three calcium-magnesium, and two zinc tablets. After procrastinating a few minutes with every excuse I could think of, I took my first sip. Then, I would take a sip, hold it in my mouth while I shuddered, and then swallow. I had to talk myself through each swallow. As I finished the last sip, I smiled, glad that the torture was over until the next morning. Feeling a little queasy, I retired for the evening, not knowing if I would wake up.

The next morning I cheerfully woke up. I was able to eat food again. The thought of a real meal was very exciting even though I was not hungry. As I went into the kitchen to prepare breakfast, nothing sounded good, so I just had a few pieces of toast with butter and jam. After this, I drove to the beach. As with every Thursday, Siga just gave us the workout and left. My stomach was really upset, though. After a four-mile workout, I returned to Siga's. There I found almost two dozen chocolate chip cookies she had bought for me. It was a beautiful, sunny day, so I lounged on her patio soaking up the rays, eating chocolate chip cookies and drinking a glass of cool, refreshing milk. I meticulously ate the cookies, making them last for hours. I spent the afternoon reading and writing. For dinner Siga prepared spaghetti with whole wheat noodles. After dinner we piled into her van and headed to Farrell's for ice cream. I had waited all summer for this day. This was my graduation present from Siga and Hans. Unfortunately, my stomach was still not used to normal food so I could not eat that much—I only had one Super Nutty Nutty!

Friday I had a three-mile workout at 1:00 p.m. which did not go well. Then at 7:30 p.m. we went for a night swim. Before we departed, I had another protein concoction. Hans promised it would taste better, but it did not. Somehow he convinced Dan to try it, too. Then Hans filled a squirt bottle with it. He wanted us to see how it tasted while we swam.

I was very apprehensive about the workout. I really did not want to get in. I was worried something might happen. Finally, Siga noticed something was wrong. When I told her what was bothering me, she just laughed, then told Hans. He thought I was being stupid, so, then I really felt rotten. I did not like it when people made fun of me, especially when I was really serious about something.

Grudgingly, I shuffled down the hill to the beach. Syndi and Cindy were already there. Syndi had come down to watch, and Cleveland was getting in some extra credit. Casey, Siga, and Hans would be paddling for the three of us. As soon as I found out what we were doing, I ran right into the water. The water felt good, and I was not scared at all.

At the halfway point in the workout I tried to swallow some of the protein drink, but it did not go down very well at all. As soon as I finished my training and ran up the beach to get warm, I started talking to Syndi. She then told me she was not going on my crossing. I was startled and hurt. Why had she waited so long to tell me? As it was, I still had not heard any word from Jim and Bev Montrella. I still hoped they would show up at the last moment. But Syndi! I dressed without uttering another sound. I had been depressed all day, and now I felt like crying. I could not control my emotions or explain them. Quietly, I crawled into the back of the van and started crying. As Hans got in, he asked what was wrong, but I had trouble telling him. So many things were on my mind. When I got back to their house, I lay down on the couch and began to listen to a Barry Manilow record in the dark. Syndi and Dan were talking in the other room; Siga was doing some odds and ends. The mellow music made me cry even more. Siga came in and wanted to know what was going on. I told her I just wanted to relax and listen to the music; nothing was really wrong. She thought that I had had too much sugar the day before after not having it for a while, and this was causing my depression. Either way, she did not like me sitting in the dark. I knew that the depression was caused from the diet because each time I had used it before, the same thing had happened, and I liked listening to music and crying. It made me feel good.

By the next morning, I felt a lot better. I still was not my peppy self, but I pretended to be. Besides, there was one good thing about that morning—I had my last workout. I only had to swim two miles; Dan had to do three. We swam these together, then, said goodbye to each other.

As I began preparing something to eat, I dropped a glass and cut my hand in the process. So, once I cleaned up, and since I was nervous and frustrated, I decided to leave without eating. I was anxious to see my family. When my mother had come down the month before, we had gotten along very well. I was hoping everything would work out well on the swim and for her this time, too.

I waited two and a half hours for them. I was afraid something had happened. Finally, they pulled up at 3:30 p.m. after a long seven-hour drive. My mother was tired and said that she felt out of place. She wanted me to arrange a place for them, but she did not want to stay in a hotel. Why had she not told me this earlier? I thought the Yorks were extending themselves immensely by having them stay over, but my mother felt funny staying at the York's since she did not know them very well. For this reason, I thought they could spend the evening getting to know each other. They would be camping on Catalina together, so this was important. It seemed like my mother was jealous of Dottie and the friendship we had developed, and this was preventing her from even trying to get to know the Yorks.

I decided to focus my attentions on Barry, since he would be going on the boat. I wanted him to know how everything was run and who was in charge, no matter what happened. I explained that he would be helping Siga and act as a timer. He would be leaving with the boat at six or seven Sunday morning. Mr. York would be driving him, the gear, and a few other paddlers to the boat. My mother, on the other hand, would be leaving Sunday afternoon. Accompanied by Mrs. York, Barbara, and one of her friends, she would be camping at the Boy Scout camp on Catalina, just north of the Isthmus. This way she would be there for the start and the finish. If I had to land somewhere else, they would be taken to the finish. That, Siga had promised.

After I answered all their questions, I left. It was about 5:30 p.m. Since it was a warm summer evening, I put the window down, turned up the radio, and sang all the way back to Siga's.

After dinner, Siga called the York's to see how everyone was getting along. She wanted to talk to my mother and answer any of her questions. I really do not know what was said since I was told to wait in another room. That night I could not sleep, so I stayed up and watched television until I was able to fall asleep.

The next morning Siga fixed a good breakfast, but I was not hungry. I was really nervous and having doubts. Siga said she was not nervous, because she found it foolish to be nervous about a sure thing. I wondered why I could not have that much confidence in myself. I would have to learn that for the English Channel swim.

We left for the helicopter at 10:15 a.m. even though it was not scheduled to leave until 12:00 p.m.. Siga wanted to make sure nothing would go wrong. As we waited in the helicopter terminal, the Slosbergs came in. Dan was swimming on Monday evening. He asked his parents not only to be at the start, but also at the finish. This meant that after the start they would go to a local hotel, and then early the next morning they would take a helicopter to Avalon. There was not an early one to the Isthmus. As it turned out, fog delayed the helicopter, so they missed his finish by minutes.

Next, Nancy Smith, John, Syndi, and Cindy showed up full of cheer. Nancy shared chocolate chip cookies from her mom which she had brought. We spoke briefly, and a few pictures were taken. Before we knew it, the helicopter had landed. Quickly, Siga and I were ushered aboard and off we went. Behind me were my friends and safety; in front of me was the Catalina Channel. Again, I would attempt to conquer this and myself. Briefly, I contemplated my chances.

My heart was pounding as I impatiently sat in the helicopter next to Siga. I felt secure with her at my side. Nevertheless, I was sweating profusely. The ride was very pretty, hovering above the vast body of blue, flowing water. Many sailboats could be seen but they looked so tiny. I wondered what I must look like in comparison. Once we landed, we walked to the other side of the Island to our little hideaway. A friend of Siga's who had a trailer on the Island was generously letting us rest there for the afternoon. We spent over two hours speaking with him.

Within this time, I mellowed considerably. I was not as nervous or excited as I had been earlier. Siga and I sat out on the porch and ate a few sandwiches. The sun felt very good, but there was a strong afternoon breeze, which we tried to ignore. We lingered in the sun, talking about our families and what each of us would be doing in the future. After a little while, we decided to go for a short walk on the beach. The beach, as we so generously called it, was more of a rocky, shell area which led to the water. In its own strange way, it was rather pretty.

Up to this point, Siga had not discussed the swim. Now she brought it up so that we could discuss everything for the last time and then not have anything to worry about later. I had a few points I wanted to clarify, also. As we strolled along, we picked up shells and rocks. Our conversation began very casually; every aspect of the swim was covered. I wanted to make sure that the best paddler was always on my right side. I would receive all my instructions from this side, too. Again, we went over the hand signals for "stop," "faster," "slower," and "stroke count."

At one point we sat down for a minute. There was something troubling me, deep down, a fear; I had to get it out. I firmly threw a few rocks into the water as I tried to convey this to Siga. "Siga it was a long summer and I had a lot of problems. I quit many times. As I look at my overall performance, I realize that it was not very good." She interrupted, saying that that was in the past; the only thing that matters was that I had stuck it out. I nodded and slowly continued, "I am still afraid of quitting. What if it is too cold or I lose interest, or I am afraid to fight the pain? I would never be able to face you. I am afraid." She told me not to worry. She had full confidence in me. She knew I would do well and besides, she would never let me quit, no matter how tough it got. I hugged her, took a deep breath, and returned to the trailer.

I was not very excited, but maybe that was a good sign, since I would need all of my energy for the crossing. No need worrying about it anymore anyway, either. I attempted to sleep for a while, but I could not. Inevitably, we started talking again; our conversation covered a whole array of subjects from school to our love lives. It was enlightening and made me feel closer to her. She was and always had been more than a coach, she was a good friend. We both tried to relax, but both of us had headaches. All summer I had given her headaches, and even on the day of my swim I gave her one. We each took a few aspirin then pretended to sleep for half an hour before dinner.

After I attempted to eat dinner, we walked around for a while taking pictures of each other. Then we decided to have some ice cream, as that usually hit the spot. We were able to force ourselves to eat a double scoop apiece. While we were sitting in the snack bar, a few people walked in wearing wetsuits and a shirt. They looked really corny, and this made us laugh, but soon we could not stop laughing.

We parted company for about an hour because Paul, the lifeguard, had some odds and ends to do before the boat was scheduled to arrive. Afterwards, Siga and I went for a long walk along the beach at the Isthmus. It was fairly deserted and rather dark, and so, so peaceful. The harbor was very quiet, but filled with a variety of sailing vessels as it was Labor Day weekend. When we reached a point where we could walk no further, we sat down on a large, slimy rock. I took the opportunity to thank Siga for her assistance these past three years, and told her what I thought about her and that I wanted her to come to England the following summer for the English Channel crossing. I hoped everything would work out so that she would be able to come. I never wanted to lose contact with her and Hans. We had been through so much together. She agreed. She felt the same way. At this point I started crying and so did she. Deep down, I knew that this swim would be our last together if something unexpectedly came up in next year. Neither of us wanted that. For a few minutes, we were both silent.

As it was time to meet Paul at the dock, we started back. Neither of us said very much on the walk back; at least, not with words. Our silence said more than words ever could. I remember thinking, *I have to do well tonight after all I have put this woman through this summer.*

We met Paul at the rock wall overlooking the beach and the harbor. Our conversation was short and meaningless. Siga gave my arms and legs a quick rubdown, reminding me constantly to stay warm. Slowly the minutes ticked away. At 9:30 p.m., we walked up to the dock. *The Atlantis*, which Mickey had rented for the swim, would pick us up at ten o'clock; the swim would begin at eleven o'clock. I only had one and a half hours to go. It was too late to back out, but who wanted to? I was ready. I could feel it.

We sat on a storage box on the upper layer of the pier, watching all the people. Every few minutes the water taxi would arrive with another boatload of people. Most of them were fairly inebriated. Some could barely make it up the gangway. Then, two private boats tried to unload a few people at the dock. One pilot took over five minutes to maneuver his boat into the dock.

At 9:45 p.m., some of Siga's friends who worked on the Island came to talk to us. They could not comprehend what I was attempting to do, but they knew if Siga had anything to do with it, it would be a success. They were very friendly and stayed with us until the boat arrived. As we chatted, the boat could be seen in the distance. At that instant, I told Siga I had forgotten my cap and goggles and started to leave. She laughed as she grabbed me and pretended to force me down the plank to the lower dock. We both laughed and I said, "It's time to conquer the Channel."

As the boat approached, I thought how large it looked. Most of the people seemed to be on the deck. A few yelled as I prepared to climb aboard. Standing in front of me was Syndi Goldenson. Goldie. She came after all! That turkey! I could not believe it. I was excited. Quickly, I climbed aboard. As I hugged her, she told me that she would not have missed it for anything. I next said hello and thank you to each of my paddlers, timers, helpers, and the crew as the boat pulled away from the dock. We were heading to Doctor's Cove. While the paddlers were receiving their final instructions, I walked to the front of the boat. I needed a second by myself. I gazed towards the mainland, then to the Island and back. It did not look that far. At first, the water looked calm, but then I realized there was a swell. I could feel the breeze also. As I emerged from the darkness into the light of the aft of the boat, I started to get nervous. This was it. Siga awoke me from my dreaming with an order to strip; we were almost there. Siga prepared to get on the skiff as the boat halted. Slowly, I undressed, shaking hands and hugging various people as they came up to wish me luck. Hans told me to hurry up; Siga was already in the skiff. My younger brother came up and kissed me. I did not want to let him go. I was so happy and proud that he was there. Finally, I climbed into the skiff. I was standing in the front of it when we pushed away from the boat.

Going ashore in skiff in the dark to start double

Quickly we made our way through various boats that were moored in the cove. As we approached the shore, we could see twenty to thirty people standing there. Where had they all come from? They did a spell out, first my name, then Siga's. Then they said, "California, here

I come." We realized that this was a whole group of Boy Scout leaders my mother had recruited for the evening. They sang a few songs and yelled continuously. It was amazing. What a welcome party! As the boat stopped, I noticed my mother standing in front of us, taking pictures. She looked very happy and enthusiastic. I was very pleased that she was there.

Siga prepared to put the Vaseline on me while I was speaking to my mother and the others. I was not concentrating when she asked me where I needed it. In a daze, I only told her to put it under my suit straps. I totally forgot to tell her my underarms and the back of my neck! This was a senseless error on my part and the one which would cause numerous problems later and result in severe rubs.

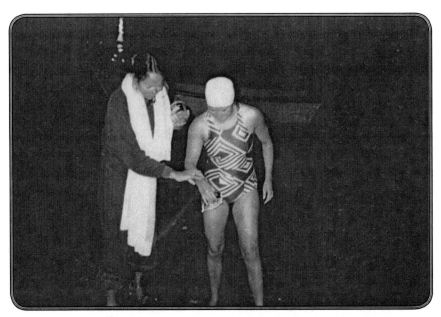

**Siga greasing my forearms instead of
underarms which didn't need it**

When Siga finished, she kissed me and got back into the skiff. The first two paddlers, Hans and Bruce, anxiously stood in the knee-deep water, waiting for the start. I tried to speak to the Scout leaders and to listen to what people were asking me, but I was not with it at all. The skiff was slowly returning to the boat, or so it seemed to me. My mother was standing off to one side. Instantly, the warning shot went off. I was standing too far from the beach; I had to move forward quickly. As I started to move, my mother attempted to grab me. Without thinking, I told her not to touch me. The only thing on my mind was to get nearer to my paddlers and the beach. I was thoughtless! Here she was reaching out to me wish to me good luck, and I pushed her away. When I realized what I had done and what she must be thinking and feeling, I started to turn around to talk to her. At that point, Hans ran up, kissed me, and told me to do it. That only made matters worse. My mind was jumping from one thing to another. As I was thinking about how much I must have hurt my mother and how much I wanted to hug her, the second shot, the starting shot, was fired. It was too late. The Scout leaders began yelling, so I carefully waddled across the rocks and into the warm, enticing water. It felt warmer than I expected. I started to turn around to say goodbye to my mother, but did not.

Start of double of Catalina

My first few strokes felt easy and long. As we made our way through Doctor's Cove, I swam over a rock, scraping my body across the top of it. We passed in between the sailboats which were showing some signs of life, probably due to all the commotion. Within a few minutes, the beach was no longer visible. Gradually, I began to pick up my pace. I could not help thinking of the agony that awaited my mother and the others on the Island. They would have no idea how I was doing, if I quit, or if I broke the halfway record. Not knowing would be very nerve-racking; it would be a long night for them.

In front of us was the boat. The skiff had been tied to the back end and moved erratically forward, in a zigzag pattern. Siga was positioned on the deck, where she remained for the next twenty hours. The boat stayed a few hundred feet in front of us until we were a mile or so from the shore. Then it slowed while I was positioned off the stern port corner of the boat. I was approximately fifteen yards from the boat. At this point, everyone was still on the deck, standing near the rail. They were yelling incessantly as I caught the boat. Within minutes, quite a few of them disappeared. It looked like it was going to be a long night and day.

Initially, my strokes felt good, but they never really felt powerful. That little extra just was not there, but after my summer, what could I expect? At the first stroke count, my strokes were eighty-eight per minute. To relay this information to me, the paddler on my right showed me a closed fist, the signal for stroke count. Then when I breathed to that side again, he yelled out, "Eight." On the next breath to his side, he yelled the second number, which in this case, was also an eight. This was repeated twice, or until I nodded my head in an affirmative manner to acknowledge that I had heard it. I retained this pace for quite a while.

As I had noticed earlier, the water was not calm. There was a long swell hitting from the left side. The wind was up, also. I began to realize that my right underarm was aching; it seemed to be sticking. That was when I realized my earlier mistake. What a stupid oversight! I had forgotten to have Vaseline put there. Skin was rubbing on skin. I needed Vaseline desperately, but I postponed asking for it until the pain became unbearable. I thought I could make it to the two-hour mark, but I could not. I had to take care of it before it was too late. But I was afraid to stop—I was racing the clock, and the clock never stops. Finally, I rose up my courage and asked for it, but I continued swimming until I was given the signal to stop.

I watched Hans relay the message. Bruce quickly paddled over, picked up the jar, then gave it to Hans and went back. Once Bruce was back in place, Hans signaled me to stop. He began to put it on his hands. He told me to come closer and he would put it on. Shocked, I said, "No way. If you touch me, I will be disqualified." I told him to give me the jar. Once I had the jar, I put a lot on, covering my right underarm, but still did not think to put it on the left one. I did not have any pain there, so I did not think of it. I still cannot believe how disoriented, absent-minded, and illogical I became during the Catalina Channel crossing. My mind only concentrated on a few things unless my body started to complain of pain. Because I had Vaseline all over my hands, I was handed a towel. This break had taken over six minutes. That error prevented me from breaking eight hours thirty minutes on the one-way and twenty hours on the double. Every second counts.

Quickly, I started again. My first thought was that the pair of goggles I had on was fine. I remember thinking, *Thank goodness I do not have the leaking goggles problem of last year.* (Too bad there was not a piece of wood for me to knock on.) Nothing else was bothering me. I actually felt good. I was getting a little bored, so I began watching the people on the boat. As time wore on, more people went below. It was interesting to watch who was talking with whom, who was still awake, who had left the deck first, who stayed up, and what those who were still visible were doing. In the wee hours of the night the deck was deserted except for three people, Barry, Syndi, and Siga. They remained awake throughout the swim, much to my amazement. Sometimes Barry would lean over the side, just above me, wave, yell, or make funny faces. He supported me a great deal, which further inspired me. *That is my younger brother up there!* I was so pleased he was able to come along.

It was especially fascinating to watch Siga. She was wearing a blue ski jacket similar to my brother's. Unlike the other two, who walked around, she barely moved more than ten feet or so. She did not yell much, but she was always there, either watching my stroke or counting it. We attempted to maintain eye contact; it made both of us feel much closer.

I really enjoyed looking at the people. It kept my mind off the swim. Besides, I always knew they were there if I needed them. That was a good feeling. I also did things to lighten everyone's spirits. I would smile, stick out my tongue, or laugh when people motioned to me. Anything to stay in a good mood, not to think about what I was doing, how far I had gone, how much my arms ached, or the pain.

The first two hours went very, very slowly. To myself I pondered, *Aren't two hours up yet? If this is only two hours, it will be a long swim!* My stroke still was not correct, either. It was effortless, but it was not fast enough or as powerful as it should have been. I tried to concentrate on it as much as possible.

I divided part of my mind to watch the people on the boat, part to think about my stroke, and the other part was able to daydream, sing songs, write a story and/or plan my future. The mind can do many things at once. I had spent many years developing this skill so that I could practice and write school papers or do schoolwork at the same time.

I always knew when it was time for me to stop, because the paddlers would change first. Once the replacement paddlers were in position, I was able to stop. At this first exchange, I watched intently. Bruce paddled over to the skiff. While he got off, Casey climbed on board. Then Casey paddled over and positioned himself on my left. At this time, Hans waved goodbye, and proceeded to the skiff where Mike Norris was waiting. Quickly, Mike climbed aboard and aligned himself on my right side. Once both of them had warmed up, Mike gave me the signal to stop. The exchange had gone very smoothly, at least from my viewpoint. I was very close to the boat when I stopped. Siga was right above me. She told me to slow down, my stroke count was still at eighty-eight, and that was too fast. I had a long way to go. She did not want me to burn out. She suggested that I slow to eighty-two strokes per minute instead. That would not take very much effort to maintain. A squirt bottle of ERG was thrown to me. I drank a quarter of the contents, approximately four ounces, relieved my system of some extra fluids, and prepared to continue. As I started up again, the people on the deck came alive with encouragement. Hans and Bruce stayed on the deck for a few minutes, removing their wetsuit tops and drying off. After this, they went below to sleep.

For the next two hours, I kept my stroke count at eighty-four. Below me there was a lot of movement. I could see a few stingrays floating along, and jellyfish bobbing up and down. At this point, however, the latter remained approximately fifteen feet under the surface. Thank goodness I was not getting stung! The light from the boat also attracted numerous varieties of small sea life. Every once in a while I would catch a glimpse of a bigger fish. I did the most sensible thing I could; I closed my eyes until the danger passed. Actually, there was not that much danger. If a shark happened to appear, which was very likely at night, the scanners on the boat would have picked it up. Then the navigator would do one of two things, each of which worked equally well—he either revved the engine to frighten the fish, or he cut off the shark's path. Whenever a large unidentified fish was spotted, the paddlers were instructed to move as close to the boat as possible. Then they were supposed to move in so the swimmer would barely have room to swim without hitting their boards. On neither of my crossings did this need to be done. The bigger fish did not like me. Yay!

Some of my teammates were not as lucky. During Cindy Cleveland's swim in October, numerous sharks were spotted. At one point, a shark came very close and continued to return in spite of numerous maneuvers. Finally, she was stopped and the crew prepared to pull her out. Meanwhile, the shark was gaffed, but was dropped while being pulled on board. Luckily, dolphins appeared on the horizon and her shark problems were soon over.

The replacement paddlers were very enthusiastic and supportive. Every few minutes they yelled something. They smiled continuously. Casey gave me okay signals, while Mike smiled, clapped, and yelled, "Good!" Boy, were those two good looking! So many times I wanted to reach out and grab them. I was lucky because all of my paddlers were good looking as well as excellent paddlers. Anything to make you happy and swim faster certainly helps!

Sometime during those two hours I was stung on my right shoulder by a jellyfish. It burned with agonizing pain for half an hour.

We had to get out of the path of a tugboat, so the second feeding was delayed fifteen minutes. It was 3:15 a.m. when I finally stopped. I wanted to know how far I had gone. I felt okay; the pace was a little too easy, and nothing was hurting too much. After a quick drink, I began again, without ever learning how far I had gone.

Up to that point, I had remained on the port side of the boat, near the rear corner. I was always within view of the people on the deck. Again, I enjoyed being there, because I could see everyone. However, the navigator began making some changes that prevented me from maintaining this contact. He would pull the boat ahead so I was left in the darkness, behind the boat and the attached skiff. There I smelled the stench from the engine, the exhaust. Then the boat seemed to idle while I not only caught up, but would pull ahead of it into the darkness. For a while I would remain in this darkness. Many memories of the swim the year before emerged, but *Why was he doing this?* was the only thought on my mind. I really did not like the situation then, either, but I was not as afraid as I had been the previous year. When Siga realized what was happening, she had someone hold a light over me while I was isolated in front of the boat. She must have known from my erratic strokes how I felt, besides remembering my discomfort the year before. As the time wore on, however, I became very aggravated with the situation.

The next thing I knew, the third set of paddlers, Brian and Gary, were in for their first time. Soon, Brian, who was on my right, was getting too far in front of me. As soon as I stopped to eat, Siga corrected him before I had a chance to protest my discomfort. He did much better after that. The last set of paddlers was Dick Yeo and Paul. They were always too far from the boat. I wanted to hug its side. I tried to tell Paul this, but he either did not comprehend, or he had other instructions. Unsuccessfully, I tried to force him over, but he would not budge, and that bothered me. All of a sudden, it seemed to be getting lighter. Furthermore, I was cold. That had to mean I was within the area of the continental shelf. *But could I still be so far from the halfway point of my swim?* I wondered what time it was and if I still had enough time to break the one-way record set by Mary Beth just two weeks earlier.

After a while, Hans and Bruce were back in. *Had eight hours really gone by?* I still could not see the shore, nor could I believe I was not in yet. I should have finished within eight hours; something must have gone wrong. Maybe the paddlers had not gone two hours each. After fifteen minutes, I had a break. Siga said I had an hour and four minutes before the record. That meant it had to be 6:29 a.m. She told me to go for it if I wanted it, but not to tire myself for the return. As I took off again, I tried to pick it up. I was pretty disgusted. I had wanted to swim a lot faster. I tried to go faster, but I could not. The cold water was beginning to have an effect on me. I felt tired; my legs were cramping, too.

The deck was no longer empty. Almost everyone was topside, trying to encourage me. A dense fog covered us; the atmosphere was very eerie. Gradually, the shoreline became visible. It seemed to be lurking off to my port side. It was rather foreboding. I could have sworn I was swimming parallel to the shore! This feeling was confirmed when I passed the point of Marineland and continued on into the beach by the dock. Instead of landing at the nearest point, I was finishing at the safest place. Siga was more concerned that I not get hurt on the entry than she was about my halfway time. If I had stopped at the nearest point, I would have finished at least thirty minutes earlier. Obviously, I wanted the faster record instead of the safer finish, but Siga was right!

The boat stopped about 400 yards from shore. The skiff was lowered, and I could see Siga being rowed toward shore. As I passed the boat, everyone was standing, yelling frantically. Then, Hans, Bruce, and I took a 90° turn, pointing me directly at the beach. Quickly, I lifted my head; I was a little disoriented. Dead ahead 300 yards was the beach. There had to be twenty to thirty people standing on the beach in front of me. Cautiously, I swam in through the waves, leaving Hans and Bruce behind. Miraculously, I timed the waves perfectly. I let a breaking wave push me into shore. Then, as it began to recede, I grabbed hold of a rock. As the water disappeared, I attempted to stand.

Awkwardly, I staggered up the rocks to the beach as quickly as I could. As I did this, all my friends screamed encouragements. I pulled off my goggles so I could see where I was walking. I glanced over the crowd and smiled as I plopped down in front of Siga. My side was to the beach. I was looking half at Siga and half at the point of Marineland in the distance. Immediately, Siga threw a few towels over me, without touching me. I was too cold, however; I could not stop shivering. Siga began talking to me. At this point, a long TV microphone was stuck in front of me. It recorded the conversation between Siga and me even though she tried to speak softly to prevent this from happening. I had broken Marybeth's record by ten minutes! Siga was pleased with my swim thus far; however, she wanted me to pick it up and try to negative split it, just as we had planned. My stroke was fine, but I had to work on my kick. It had faltered in the cold water, and by the end my stroke count had also dropped.

I was drinking ERG while Siga was talking to me. She tried to force me to eat a cheese sandwich, but I could not as it was so hard to chew. I was only able to eat half of one. My mouth was so sore and swollen because of the cold, salt water. The inside of my mouth was swollen and this caused pain. I did eat a few cookies, though.

As I sat there, Mrs. Goldenson came up and said a few words. I was afraid she might touch me, so I warned her not to. She smiled and said she would not. Then, Mrs. Troyer said hello. Next, my father came by; Siga had called him down. She knew I wanted to say hello to him. He had driven all the way from San Francisco to be at the halfway point. Having my dad there made me feel good and proud. I turned to the crowd and said hello to Mrs. Cleveland, Mr. York, and waved at some others. A camera was in front of Siga, and I was asked if I wanted to say anything. I did not at that time. Then Siga said, "Let's go." I took a deep breath, and then nodded my head. Mechanically, I dropped the towels and stood up. As I slowly moved towards the water, the crowd began to yell. Cautiously, I studied the waves, waiting for the right time to go. Beyond the waves, I could see Hans and Bruce sitting on their boards, clapping, and trying to stay warm. The scene on the boat was similar; they were all waving. In a mad dash, I cleared the breaking waves without any complications. As I put on my goggles, I turned briefly and waved to those on the shore. It would be a long time until I saw them again.

As I started swimming, my goggles filled with water; they did not stick. A few minutes later, I again yelled, "Let's go," as I passed the boat. I was very cold, but I hoped I would get warmer soon. Unfortunately, I never did.

After about a mile, I told Hans I needed another pair of goggles. I exchanged goggles with him, but the new ones did not stick either. After a few frustrating minutes, I angrily asked for another pair. Hans just glared, but he relayed the message to the boat. Bruce disappeared again then returned with yet another pair. I had seven pairs on the boat. I was so cold and getting more and more frustrated with each passing minute. I put on this new pair. They stuck, but they were foggy. I was so upset I just began swimming. I did not care anymore that I could not see at all. I was on the verge of crying. Over an hour had gone by.

At last I was able to stop and eat. To everyone's amazement, I asked for my first pair of goggles. I could tell that the general attitude was a little apprehensive. They were worried. Siga told me to relax and to get back into it. It would work out soon. While I ate, the paddlers were switched. As I began swimming again, I was moved to the other side of the boat. Paul jumped in to pace me. A pace swimmer helps you swim faster. With the clean goggles, I could see again. As an added bonus, Mike was next to me. Mike was constantly shouting, "You're outstanding," or, "You are doing great!" I had to swim harder when he was there because of his efforts. He was so enthusiastic I wanted to kiss him.

I was beginning to relax; I was re-inspired. Then I saw Paul trying to catch me. I decided to take off so he would not be able to catch me. As I did, I smiled at him. It was a mean thing to do to Paul. I am afraid it demoralized him. However, he helped me swim faster, and that was the objective.

Gradually we began drifting from the boat. I was losing eye contact with Siga and the others. Suddenly, I realized the water was choppy. It was so early; that was not a good sign. I think Mike noticed my doubt and fear of the prevailing conditions. With each passing minute, the conditions were growing worse. It was only 11:00 a.m. After Mike finished paddling, he turned around, jumped in, and swam with me. *Where did he find the strength?* I really enjoyed it, but he had to be hurting terribly. Besides, he was not wearing any goggles.

During my third feeding, I had a few cookies, but I wanted more. I had already gone a little over halfway. I was just under four hours which was a record pace. It was physically possible for me to negative split the swim. I was doing really well, and getting stronger with each stroke. I had only ten miles left to go. But I also knew that the recent changing conditions would have some effect on me, but not how much. The conditions would make or break the rest of my swim. I was moved back to the left side of the boat. The chop was very bad, reaching a few feet by then. I started swallowing a lot of salt water. Gradually, my mouth was burning with pain.

At the next break, although I tried, I could not eat anything because of the pain in my throat. It hurt and the cookies and chicken scratched it. Before I had left, Siga said, "You are outstanding." I looked up at her and jokingly replied, "Yes, That's right. I would like to be—out standing." Then I smiled and took off again. Now, I was really getting hit by the chop. The water was so turbulent, it was hard to stroke properly. I was swimming up and down instead of forward. At the next break, two hours after I had been told I was halfway, Siga informed me that I only had six or seven miles left. My mouth must have dropped with my astonishment. That meant I had gone only three miles in two hours, while I had been averaging five to five and a half miles before. Yet, my stroke count had not changed, only the weather conditions had. The ocean was very rough. It was slowing me considerably. I was disappointed, but I had to stay positive, not only for me, but for everyone on the boat and on the shore at the finish, but especially for Siga.

The conditions worsened. At times there were waves over six feet high and the wind was twelve knots. The paddlers were having problems, too. They could not stay on their boards and they were doing everything possible to control them. They were not having much luck though, and soon I started getting hit by the boards. The waves were so erratic we were pushed into each other. I was very frustrated and a little perturbed. *Why couldn't they be careful?* I asked myself, knowing it was not their fault. Then they would look at me as if it were my fault. That was disturbing. The paddlers began switching at shorter intervals; then Syndi Goldenson paddled. She should not have done so with her sore arm, but she was trying to help. I was so proud of her.

My feedings were every hour now. After two more hours, Siga regretfully, but in a positive tone, told me I had four to five more miles. She hid her feelings of disappointment, but I could not. I was mad. *What was wrong?* Rudely, and with a defeatist attitude, I asked, "In two hours, I have gone only one or two miles? Will it take me five more hours to swim four to five miles?" All she could do was tell me to keep fighting. To myself I muttered, *Just try one more. Do one mile at a time; nothing else mattered. Be tough.*

Boy, was I disappointed. I knew if conditions were better I could have negative split the swim. We were drifting almost a mile south for every mile I went forward. Brian began to swim with me. Just then a Channel 4 helicopter passed overhead and circled a couple of times. I asked Siga for my makeup kit. I needed to powder my cheeks for the camera.

Brian dropped out after a while. Unexpectedly, someone else dove in. It was Mike. *Boy, I love him,* I thought. I never knew anyone to fight so hard, and he was doing this for me. I had to keep up with him; he was doing a job far beyond what I or anyone else had expected.

My muscles were aching. Worse than that was the pain I had with each breath. It hurt all the way down into my lungs. I attempted to breathe with my teeth closed, thinking it would feel better. Again the boat was pulling too far ahead. With the wind I could no longer stand the fumes. It added to the pain in my throat, and further aggravated my lungs. I also tried to stay away from my paddlers. I was tired of getting run into. Since I was tired and frustrated and nobody seemed to notice or tried to alleviate the situation, I stopped looking at Siga. Actually, nothing could be done by anyone; this was my battle with myself. I was beginning to fight the pain. It was late; the swim was taking too long.

Realizing I was letting these things affect me, I told myself to fight them. I had to; I had to keep going. I would feel better after a short break, but for some reason Siga would not let me stop.

Finally, I was able to stop. Three more miles, there were still three more miles of swimming uphill, breathing with the agonizing pain, and trying to mentally overcome the pain. Three miles. I was not relieved or happy; I just wanted to finish!

Siga informed me that the Los Angeles Lifeguard Baywatch had transferred my mother and friends to the finish at the Marine Biology Station. This was a few miles south of the Isthmus. No wonder it was taking so long. Everybody was encouraging me to keep fighting. I was tired, frustrated, but somehow, I was able to keep going.

An hour or two later, Siga stopped me and said, "Only one more mile. Just try one more." She and Syndi were yelling, "Do it. Go now." The paddlers switched again. Hans and Bruce were back in the water for the last time. Just before I left, Siga told me I would be landing at the rock quarry, still farther south. I did not have to worry about my mother either; she was there already. I could see the massive shore off to my port. We were moving parallel to the shore again to reach a place where I could easily land. My only thoughts were, *Come on, let's land.* Then Mike dove in again. How could I show my disappointment when he was in there again? He never ran out of energy or enthusiasm; he gave 100 percent.

Another boat was approaching and blowing its siren. I could also see my brother climbing into the skiff. *But where was Siga? Why was she still on the boat?* Again, she had not paddled or swum, but surely she would meet me on the beach. *She had to be at the finish; she just had to.*

I looked up. There was the beach. I could even see my mother. Mike stayed with me until the last hundred yards. The Baywatch was sounding its siren. I was almost done; I had actually made it. I did not quit, nor was there any time that I seriously wanted to. Hans and Bruce dropped back. At that moment, I saw the bottom, just fifteen feet below me. Then the rocks moved closer and closer until I touched the bottom with my hand. I started to stand up, but I could only crawl a few feet until I was out of the water. Then I was able to stand. Slowly, I took my three official steps clearing the water's edge, and fell into Siga's waiting arms. I leaned over and grabbed my mother. That was the moment I had waited for; I had made it and my mother was there.

Instantly, the reporters moved in and started asking questions. There were two TV crews on the Island for the finish. After I had answered their questions, which was very difficult since my tongue was swollen, Siga ushered me back to the skiff. She also directed my mother to it. Unfortunately, we had to sit at opposite ends. I was very cold, tired, and disoriented. All I wanted was a warm shower. Before Siga left the boat, she had instructed Syndi to make sure I had a shower, dressed, and ate something.

When the skiff reached the boat, someone lifted me out. Briefly, I said a few words to some of the people as Syndi was directing me towards the shower. I did not even see if my mother had made it aboard. I was too tired and unaware of most of the things going on around me and being said. I was done; I had made it. That was all I cared about.

I could barely stand in the shower. I kept trying to close my eyes, but Syndi would not let me. My neck and underarms were burning. I had problems taking off my cap since the cap had rubbed a deep gash into my neck. There was a lot of blood. My left underarm was covered with rub marks, all because I forgot where I needed the Vaseline. (It would take over two weeks for these to heal, and I still have a few scars in remembrance.) After the shower, I was shuffled below to dress. Nancy and my mother joined us. Mom began to tell me about her adventures on the island. She also told me about all the pictures she had taken and said that she wanted to take a few more. I was still cold, so I put on three layers of clothes. Once I was dressed, I went upstairs to meet everyone. Siga and Hans had already gone to bed since Dan's single swim would begin not long after we returned. I was offered a glass of champagne which I readily accepted. As I took a sip, my throat burned with pain, my eyes watered, and I almost choked to death. I agreed to have a bowl of ice cream instead. It sounded more appealing, anyway. Mike came and sat next to me at the Captain's table. I really enjoyed him. I was tired and kept dropping my spoon into my ice cream. Mike would reach over, pick it up, and give it back to me. After this happened three or four times, I gave him my ice cream.

During this time I spoke briefly with my brother, my mother, and most of my crew. Nancy had kept the log. Since I had never read mine from the year before, I was curious what it said. Nancy got it for me and I began to read it. I did not read much before I fell asleep.

The next time I woke up, only Nancy and Casey were sitting at the table. I could not open my eyes. My eyelids were stuck together. As soon as I finished clearing them, I fell asleep again. The last time I woke up, we were only twenty minutes from port. I chatted with the people in the room, then with my mother when she came into the room.

By that time the boat was approaching the dock. Someone from the deck told me to prepare to meet my public because they were waiting. As I emerged from the cabin, I could see thirty or more people standing on the dock, waving. There were numerous reporters, also. I walked to the stern of the boat and spoke to each of them for a few minutes.

Wonderful red roses and large crowd

Mrs. Cleveland presented me with a dozen roses. She had met my father and talked with him. During his ride home, he had been calling every hour to find out how I was doing. Mary Beth was there as she was leaving on Dan's crossing that evening. I apologized for breaking her record; she just smiled. The press came aboard for interviews. Mrs. Sonnichson also came aboard as she had arranged for members of the wire services to take pictures. She wanted Mickey, Siga, Dan, and me in the pictures; this way they could kill two birds with one stone.

While we were sitting around the table having these pictures taken, my mother walked into the room. The look on her face almost made me cry. I could see the disappointment written there. She had been left out again. I felt rotten; why had I not asked for her? I blew it. I had not introduced her to Mrs. Sonnichson, either. I owed that to her and my brother, but they were left out. That was the last I saw of my mother until I got off the boat to answer a phone interview. As I returned to the boat, I could see her sitting on the corner of the dock by herself. She was very disappointed. *Why was I so thoughtless and she so sensitive?* She had started my career, supported me both monetarily and mentally, and received very little for it. In her eyes, that was my mistake. I still hadn't got it right.

I told her I would be ready in a few minutes, as soon as I picked up my chart. She asked me when I was going to call my family; I should call them. First, although I could not tell her, I knew that my father would have already told them. Second, I wanted to be totally in on what was going on at the moment to thank everyone, and to say goodbye.

Finally, we were ready to leave. Nancy, who was also staying at the York's, drove back with us. We arrived just minutes after the news ended at 11:33 p.m. John had waited up for us to return. My swim had been the cover story on the *11 O'clock News*, even before President Carter. That made me feel pretty good. I had three calls from reporters which I had to return right after I called the rest of my family. They did indeed already know; my father had told them. It was midnight before I finished all the calls. By then, Nancy had gone to bed, as had Mr. York and John. Dottie had gone to watch the start of Dan's swim. Barry, my mother, and I stayed up to talk. At one o'clock, Barry went to bed. He had to catch a plane the next morning at nine and be at work at 10:30 a.m.

My mother and I continued talking until three in the morning. Many things had upset her, and she was angry. I had made numerous errors again. After I explained all my actions to her, we went to bed. Originally, she had planned to stay with me for a few days, and then we were going to drive home together. I had a few loose ends to tie up before I left, however. She decided that she did not want to wait around and she would leave in the morning. Even as she drove off at seven o'clock the next morning, she was still very disappointed in me for leaving her out of the pictures. She didn't like how anything went again. After driving my brother, Barry, to the airport, she returned home.

Rethinking the swim, I decided that I should have started at 5:00 p.m.. This would have helped with the return half of the swim. Of course, that is for another swimmer to do to swim it faster.

I did not go home until Friday, September 16. Behind me lay my friends, my teammates, and my life for four years. In front of me was uncertainty—with a little time at my mother's home, and then a trip to Europe for a year. I was excited about what lay ahead.

THE WATSON FELLOWSHIP

T hose last few weeks of preparation rapidly dwindled away amidst packing, planning, and goodbyes. I even went to a psychologist to plan my affirmations. I used them to plan to break the record and to deal with the pain. My flight was scheduled to depart from Oakland Airport at 4:00 p.m. Saturday afternoon, October 1, 1977. A few days before my scheduled departure, while inquiring about luggage allowance, I was informed that the charter company was on strike. The new flight had been scheduled to leave at 10:00 p.m. from San Francisco. I would be flying on either TWA or United.

My older brother, Brian, and his wife, Chris, decided to organize a family get-together on the Saturday I left. I had not seen my father since the halfway point of my double swim, and I wanted to say goodbye. Unfortunately, he had left town the day before I arrived back in Northern California.

Brian arranged for me to see Dad the afternoon of the party. Brian's plan was simple. He would act as a decoy by going shopping, taking mom, Carolyn, and Ron (her husband) along. Meanwhile, Chris would drive me over to see my dad and have me back before the others returned. A snag developed, however, when Mom agreed to go shopping only after asking if I would also go. I hesitated long enough for her to say she did not want to go unless I did. This was reasonable, since we only had a few hours left together, and she wanted to spend all of it with me.

Reluctantly, I agreed, knowing full well I had to remain behind, or I would not see my father for another year. As Brian prepared to leave, Carolyn distracted Mom while I slipped into the backyard. Quickly, they piled into the car and left before Mom realized I was not coming. As soon as we were sure that they had left, Barry, Kelly, Chris, and I rushed to the seaside café where Dad had waited all afternoon for me to come for a quick visit. As we arrived, he was leaving. He left his car, and I ran up and hugged him. His face looked tired and worn. There was more gray in his hair than the last time I'd seen him. I just felt like holding him; I could not speak. He spoke of my Catalina swim and my upcoming adventure. As always, he warned me to be careful, but to enjoy myself completely. The time passed so quickly. The others were worried and thought we had better leave. I wanted to stay, to hold this man, to talk with him, but I knew I had to leave. My heart swelled with pain on our final goodbye.

Quietly, I returned to the car, watching Dad ease into his car. I could not help feeling sad. He must be so lonely. On the ride back to the house, I questioned marriage. Together, my parents were not happy, and apart each had a void. I only hoped each would find something or someone to fill their emptiness. (At the time, I didn't know of my father's twelve-year love affair or that he was happy!)

Upon returning to the house, I was very depressed. I was overjoyed at having seen my father but depressed at the way I had to see him, and sad at having to say goodbye. Soon after the others arrived, this mood quickly subsided. Mom could not understand why I had not gone shopping, so I made up some trivial excuse. I knew she would be hurt if she knew where I had gone, and I did not want her to be upset.

The rest of the afternoon went well. Around six o' clock, I bid goodbye to Brian, Chris, Barry, and Kelly, and with the others, I departed for the airport. After numerous check-ins and arrangements, the four of us were sitting in the gate area. Little was said. I was nervous. It was October 1, and I would not return until August 22 of the following year, just in time for law school to begin. There was a possibility I would postpone law school. Or would I? It all seemed so far away.

At 9:30 p.m., my thoughts were disturbed when it was announced that the plane was ready for boarding. *What was I getting into?* Briefly, I hugged Mom, Carolyn, and Ron. As I turned to leave, my knees started shaking. I staggered a few steps, made a 180° turn, and grabbed my mom again. I loved her so very much; I knew I would miss her, despite all our conflicts. She hugged me tightly. Quickly, I walked the long corridor without glancing back. A few minutes later, the plane was circling the Bay, passing the Golden Gate. Twelve years earlier I had swum there. That failure had encouraged me to keep going—to someday swim the English Channel and break the record for my mother. Within the year, I would meet that challenge.

San Francisco to New York; New York to Frankfurt, Germany; from there, I had to travel by train to Bonn, the capital of Germany and also the home of SSF Bonn—the best swim club in Germany. Due to a six-hour delay in New York, our plane touched ground in Frankfurt at 10:50 p.m. on Sunday, October 1. Everything was closed. I could not exchange money, so I could not buy a train ticket. Finally, I figured out I could change money at one of the local hotels. I was able to exchange money and bought a ticket to Bonn, leaving at 2:10 a.m. and arriving at 6:30 a.m. For two hours I rested, then boarded the train. I entered a cabin in which another passenger was lying down. Since I had a four-hour journey, I intended on doing the same. He offered to wake me when we arrived in Bonn. A bit apprehensive, but very exhausted, I drifted into a light sleep. One town, then another slowly passed by. I kept a sleepy eye on our progress.

Then, without any notice, the man was calling, "This is Bonn." Bonn! I jumped up, grabbed my suitcases, and jumped off the train just as it began to pull away. Relieved that I had made it, I surveyed my surroundings. Immediately, I realized my error. This was not the right station; it was too small. This station was Bonn—Bad Godesburg, the American military town. Bonn was a major city five miles down the track, and the right stop.

The platform was deserted except for my bright pink suitcase, my brown Speedo case, and Speedo shoulder bag. The air was very cold; it was dark and overcast, with a light drizzle. I was cold; my coat was not warm enough. Then it dawned on me—I was in Germany, thousands of miles from home and friends. I was alone with only a few German marks in my possession, and at the wrong station. I did not speak a word of German beyond the courtesies, and it was raining. I looked up and smiled—this would be a year I would never forget. Fortunately, I caught the next train to Bonn, the capital of Germany in 1977.

During the next eight months, I would stay in Germany, Italy, Sweden, France, Belgium, Luxembourg, Switzerland, Ireland, and England. Little did I know or realize how much I would learn in that time not only about swimming, the countries and the people, but especially about myself. It was time to find out who I was, why, and where I wanted to go. I also learned to deal with all types of people. These encounters aided me in reevaluating myself, my ideals, and my lifestyle. I am extremely grateful to the Watson Foundation for the opportunity I was given which led to my being able to travel to all of these countries and to meet and work with so many wonderful people.

My goal was to analyze various swimming programs in these countries and then to compare my findings with such programs in the United States. Furthermore, I prepared to swim the English Channel and then write a book on my marathon swimming career. In the eleven and a half months I spent in Europe, from October 2 to September 15, 1978, I trained with over twenty swimming clubs. These ranged from the national clubs in West Germany, Sweden, Luxembourg, and Belgium, to strong, private clubs in various other countries. Likewise, almost all of the coaches were the national coaches, whereas only a few were soon to be the national coaches. I also had the opportunity to speak with the swimmers, coaches, officials, and sport doctors, not only from these Western European countries but from some Eastern countries as well.

My itinerary was as follows:

October 1—November 30, 1977	Bonn, West Germany
December 1—December 15	Rome, Italy
December 15—December 23	Wurzburg, West Germany
December 23—December 31	Giessen, West Germany
January 1—February 8, 1978	Borlänge, Sweden
February 8—February 12	Paris, France
February 13—March 5	Liege, Belgium
March 5—March 20	Eeklo, Belgium
March 20—March 31	Luxembourg, Luxemburg
April 1—April 30	Zürich, Switzerland
May 1—May 28	Dinard, France
May 28—August 3	Folkestone, England
August 3—August 6	Windermere, England
August 6—August 28	London and toured Scotland
August 28—September 12	Ireland

Throughout Europe, any time I could train in open water, I did. I was in the Atlantic Ocean in November, the Mediterranean Sea in December, and in many small lakes and rivers throughout the year. The water was often very cold—probably too cold for most swimmers. I think most people who saw me swimming thought I was crazy. In Italy I swam in the Mediterranean and all the men in a nearby restaurant came out to watch me swim. When I emerged from the cold water, they gave me hot coffee and bread.

Initially, I lived for two months in Bonn, Germany with four Olympians: Karina Bormann, Stibbi Konnecker, Walter Kusch, and Angela Steinbeck. The apartment was paid for by the German National Team, as was their food and other expenses. This was 1977, long before the USA started helping Olympians at this level.

The German coach I had expected to train with had moved to the United States, so the SSF Bonn Club was coached by Rudy Spoor from South Africa. The training involved a morning practice and an evening one. As I was just getting back in the water, this was sufficient. These athletes also loved to camp and surf besides swimming. I went camping with them, and while they surfed, I swam in the ocean twice a day for two days.

I gained weight in Germany because at 4:00 p.m. every day we had cake or toast with Nutella. Afterwards, we had an evening workout (but apparently not enough to offset the effect of the cake and toast!). The weekend before I left for Rome, the women on SSF Bonn threw me a cake party. Every swimmer brought their family recipe and we ate cake for five hours.

While training in Germany, I had the privilege to meet with Dr. Madeo, a sports doctor who had escaped from East Germany when it was controlled by the communists and taught at the University of Koln. He answered over twenty questions in the hour I met with him. He explained to me how the East Germans, Russians, and other Eastern women passed the doping test in 1976. A small bag of someone else's urine was implanted in the woman's uterus. When they were tested, all they had to do was reach in and pop the bag. It wasn't until the 1984 Olympics when they started having a person watching during the tests that this finally became known. None of these countries attended the Los Angeles Games because of the late warning of the new testing procedure.

During this time in Germany, I also lectured at numerous high schools and wrote a few articles on both life in America and my marathon swimming career. It was an excellent experience. Besides studying and training, I was able to compete in a few international meets. These included a meet in Sweden, the Tilt International in Paris, and a few smaller meets.

The second country I visited was Italy, and specifically to work with Olympic distance medalist Novella Calligaris. The training was in a twenty-five-meter bubble pool. Novella was an excellent coach. I was colder in Italy than in any other country as they never turned on the heat. Breakfast was after morning practice; then we napped, had a night practice, and ate dinner around 10:00 p.m.

At Christmastime, I spent three days in Giessen with my former college roommate prior to going to Borlänge, Sweden. It was wonderful to catch up with someone from home, and we concluded that life beyond college and our starry-eyed illusions were not the same.

Siga called me while I was in Germany. I asked her if my mother could go on the boat. She said no. My brother and the Smith family would be allowed, but not Mom. I would have to tell my mother, and I was not looking forward to it. Siga and I had a good conversation, otherwise. I was looking forward to seeing her.

Next, I spent five weeks in Borlänge, Sweden, with lots of snow and great people. We had hard workouts twice a day, maybe 15,000 meters each. Afterwards, we sat in the sauna. Then I would walk to the bus, a half mile away. I wouldn't get cold, because the buses were heated. When I arrived at the house of the family I was staying with, I would put on shorts as it was always 80° inside. One night, we went to a hockey game in a blizzard. It was freezing outside (-40° Celsius). It was outrageously cold, but a lot of fun and laughs. Our toughest workout was a straight 10,000 meter for time; I loved it.

The next country was Belgium. This country is divided into two sides—French and Flemish. I trained with Lucien Pirson of the Mosa Swim Club on the French side. In between practices, we would go to the World War I and II historic sites and the wonderful bakeries. One night after my third practice, I had a sweet hamburger meat sandwich, only to be told it was horsemeat. I almost threw up, but, ironically, I really liked it.

One day, I did a 25,000 meter swim. When I left the water, my left shoulder was blue and my fingers were numb. I had a lot of pain and realized that it had never hurt this much before. I wasn't sure what to do, so I just decided to ignore it for a while.

Next, I stayed three weeks in Eeklo, Belgium training with Herman VerBowwen. We trained very hard. For respite, I traveled to Bruge for linen and experienced tongue for dinner one night. Not only was I learning the training techniques, but I was sharing in a few habits and customs of my fellow swimmers.

Next was Luxemburg for two weeks. I stayed with the national coach. I turned 23 while I was there, and we had a big club party. My shoulder was still hurting and after I mentioned this to the group, someone told me of a good doctor in Switzerland I should see. The

Luxemburg team swam only once a day and then did a long weight session. This routine rested my shoulder somewhat.

In Switzerland, I trained with Steve Genter, a former Lakewood Aquatic Club swimmer and Olympian medalist. I stayed with the Hagelis, a swimming family of Steve's, for the month of April. They were very supportive, but this turned out to be a setback month, both physically and mentally.

Ten months earlier the English Channel swim was a dream. In April, the dream was almost shattered. One thing after another occurred.

First, Siga advised me by tape that she would be unable to come for my Channel crossing. She was pregnant and the baby was due in August. Her not coming was very disappointing. I was very pleased for her, of course; it just took a while to accept. I wanted her to be there with me. So, I decided to travel to England to see my mom. She and Aunt Olga were going on an eight-week bus tour through Europe. Once there, I asked Mom to cut her trip short to learn how to be my coach, and to meet me in Dinard, France instead. I told her I would teach her everything she needed to know.

Second, the twenty-four-hour swim I had planned was cancelled. This would have entailed attempting to swim more than sixty-one kilometers, the existing world record, in a fifty-meter pool, within that time period. My goal was one hundred kilometers. The swim was set to raise money for the handicapped and Siga's expenses. Unfortunately, after flying to Belgium tapered, mentally and physically prepared to swim, I was informed that it was postponed. Worse, there had been a mix-up and it was rescheduled for May, but nobody told me.

After returning to Switzerland from England, I decided to have my left shoulder checked. For years I had had pain in it, but it was worse now. In addition, a blue patch formed on my upper arm each time I trained, and the arm was beginning to throb. The doctor's diagnosis was that I had periarthritis—similar to tennis elbow. He suggested that I quit swimming permanently.

It was too much to handle in one month. I took a week off from training so that I could have time to gather my senses. Then, I began preparations for the Channel crossing! I officially ended my Watson study after Switzerland. Now, I could focus on the Channel swim.

Instead of studying in Ireland, I arranged to be in Dinard, France for a month. Although I planned to stay there for only a week, it would give me an opportunity to train in the North Sea. After three setbacks in April, I felt that I needed to begin the long and tedious acclimation process, regardless of the temperature or conditions. I had to be 100 percent confident of my own ability.

Once I arrived in Dinard, France I began my ocean training. Gradually, I increased my water time from five minutes to an hour and fifty minutes. When I first began, the water temperature was 47°. The tide moved in and out an unbelievable amount. I had to train as the tide was coming in as this made the walk shorter at the end of the swim when my fingers were frozen and curled and walking was difficult. By the end of May, the water temperature had reached 51°. After I swam in the ocean, I took a twenty-minute hot shower, then swam at least a two-hour pool workout. After this, I started to feel my arms and legs again. At the same time, I increased my mileage in the pool to prepare for the Channel.

My mother canceled her trip to Ireland, and came to Dinard to help me for the whole month of May. I needed someone to take times and to push me when I slowed down or when I didn't want to train. For the first time in my life, though, I didn't have any days like that. I also needed someone to help me stand after the ocean workout. Mom fulfilled this need, and helped my spirits tremendously. We became closer than we had been in years.

With Mr. Meslier, the coach of the CREN swimmers in Dinard, I arranged to swim 36,000 meters in their fifty-meter pool. I wanted to attempt to break my 1976 record of eight hours, thirty-two minutes. Furthermore, I needed the swim not only to test my speed and endurance, but for my confidence. At 2:00 p.m. on May 27, with the help of the Dinard and CREN swimmers and supporters, I completed the 720 lengths in eight hours, eleven minutes, sixteen seconds; a new world record by twenty-one minutes. Tired, but not exhausted, I spent half the night analyzing my splits and discussing the swim with my mother. My slowest 100 meter was 1:23.3. I only swam two laps of 100 meters over 1:23.0. My average was 1:21+. I began and finished in 1:16.0. Likewise, my first 1500 meters was 19:30; my last was 20:00.

Clock start

USA flag, with times on board

Finish with three pacers

The next day we packed for England—the last stage of the journey. For thirteen years, I had waited to swim the English Channel; only two months separated me from my goal. May had been a good month.

The Watson study had been very beneficial. As for my analysis, I came up with some startling evidence which held true throughout Europe. Some of this is as follows:

Advantages of swimming in Europe:

- the facilities—numerous fifty-meter pools, available 6:00 a.m.—11:59 a.m.
- free training—no dues or very little
- paid athletes—financial support $200 a month—from clubs, government
    (a) meet entry fees—also, hotel, food, and travel costs are paid
    (b) phony jobs—paid for jobs but never worked (club)
    (c) rent-free apartments—club owns
- sponsors—Volkswagen, Haribo—businesses support clubs

- equipment—wore Speedo or Arena (sponsor brands)
  (a) suits, caps, towels, sweats, shorts, bags two times a year
  (b) coaches given money to represent (Arena $10,000 per year)
- schools—special education programs only for athletes
- research—sports doctors; ear lobe test; O2 content

All of these benefits began between 1968 and 1972 due to the performances at the 1968 Olympics. The Europeans wanted to prevent another US sweep such as the one that occurred in 1968.

Disadvantages of swimming in Europe:

- attitude—athletes for money; only best in their country; family—not emphasized
- coaches—not as good; no mutual exchange as in US; no consistency in ideas or people
- long lunch break—means must begin school early and run until 4:00 or 5:00 p.m.—limits training time.

In the US, the best opportunities for swimmers were at the collegiate level. With scholarships, this is the closest the US was to achieving the advantages of the Europeans, Russians, and the Soviet Bloc countries in 1978. The question arises then, "Why does the US still do so well, especially in the men's competition?"

A few answers to this question include:

1) attitude—since there are so many athletes, one must fight to stay on top, otherwise someone else will move in.
2) coaches—again, they must perform or are out.
3) number—there are many athletes in the US.

However, I was also interested in the women. In the US, the women's high school program was mediocre and the collegiate program was non-existent on a competitive basis until 1973-74. Therefore, women swam in the AAU until they were fifteen or through high school, and then quit at eighteen. With Title IX, the US women had an opportunity to continue swimming after high school on a wide scale in the US. Thus, our poor performances in the 1972-76 Olympics were reversed. The only fear is whether or not the subsidization of athletes in the US will promote the stagnation of performance as evidenced in Europe by 1978.

Below is a brief comparison of the US and European swimming programs:

1968	US Women—Top
1969-72	Europeans improved; redeveloping US programs
1969-72	US women—no major changes
1972	US women—mediocre
1972	Europeans did well
1973-76	US women—no improvement in high school or collegiate until 1975-76
1973-76	Europeans surpassing US
1976	US women—poor performances
1977	Europeans relaxing; money beginning to influence
1977	US begins reevaluation on a large basis
1978	European and US the same

The Watson Graduate Fellowship changed my life and opened the whole world to me. I will always be indebted to them. The experiences and knowledge I gained in Europe are incomparable. The year was beneficial for my study of the many swimming programs, my marathon swimming career, my awareness of other people and their lifestyles, but especially for my own personal growth and development. The year was very useful, exciting, and extremely worthwhile.

THE FINAL LEG

Thirty hours after leaving Dinard, France, my mother and I, exhausted, climbed off the train in Folkestone, England. This would be our home for two months. The weather was unbelievable—sunny and warm. Little did we know it would be over a month until we saw the sun again; but at the time, it did not matter.

Folkestone is a beautiful city, with quaint shops, many green parks, lovely walking paths by the sea, and all with an extremely friendly atmosphere. I was bubbling with excitement as the taxi carried us through the city to our hotel. The Hotel Barrelle was situated on the Marine Parade, opposite the Rotunda Amusement Park and the ocean. It was a four-story edifice connected to ten similar establishments built in a row. The similarity ended there. This hotel was owned and run by the dynamic Mrs. Godefroy. Her mother had established it in 1913. Now, at seventy-three, Mrs. Godefroy was still doing a marvelous job, making people think she was in her late fifties. Also, there was Ms. Albert—a tiny, frail woman with more energy than a young child. At seventy-eight, she was fun to be with and concerned about her friends.

In a short time, the hotel became more of a home than a hotel. All the people, from Claire, who served our breakfast, to Pat, who cleaned our room, were concerned about my training, our welfare, our happiness, and our comfort. Due to the generosity of the management of the Folkestone Sports Center, I was allowed to train without cost in their twenty-five-meter indoor pool. Since I planned to train once or twice a day in the pool in addition to an ocean workout, I had to get up fairly early. I was given permission to use the pool from 6:45 to 8:45 a.m. I had the pool all to myself and did not have to contend with either school children or the public. The only difficulty was the distance from our hotel to the Center, which was on the far side of town. It was a good twenty-minute walk once one had climbed the 186 steps up the cliff from the hotel. Half asleep at 6:15 a.m., it was always difficult to manipulate the stairs. Then, after workout, I had to dress quickly and rush back to the hotel because the breakfast ended at 9:30 a.m.

My afternoon pool trainings were during times with the public. I gradually came to dread going in the afternoon. At times, it was a very trying situation. The pool was a popular spot for kids, and often very crowded. It was difficult to avoid being jumped upon, kicked, run into, backed into, or even lifted up while swimming a workout. Sometimes I was hit so many times I was too frustrated to continue, but I did. Many times I returned to the hotel bruised and battered, with cuts and bruises—mementos from a "hard" training. I was grateful for the opportunity to swim, so I accepted the situation and kept on. Fortunately, the lifeguards were extremely friendly and tried to alleviate the problems.

My pool and open water training was for a 200 meter event in the Olympics, lots of them but at the 200 meter speed. This was what I planned for, not a long swim pace. I needed the speed and the endurance, but it was fast speed and endurance training. The English Channel was going to be my Olympics.

As it turned out, while I was in Europe I began to write this autobiography. One day in early June, I gave it to my mom to read. When she reached the part about the Golden Gate swim, she started crying. I asked her what was wrong, and she replied that she had walked away then because she felt she had pushed me too hard and she felt guilty. She was so ashamed, she couldn't talk about it. For thirteen years, I thought I had failed her. Right then, we agreed to make the Channel swim our swim and would put everything both of us had into it. That day, the Channel swim took on new meaning. I had to succeed and break the record. I wanted it for one day. After that it didn't matter.

The sea was not crowded at all, but it was very dangerous. The water was cold—50° to 55° from May 30 to July 4, then 56° to 59° after the Gulf Stream alteration effectively warmed the area. The water was unpredictable however.

Low tide and rusty barriers visible; not visible at high tide

It was affected by the currents, tides, winds, and rain. One second it would be calm, then the wind would come up and four foot waves would be thrashing around.

Another aspect of this was the beach. Unlike a sandy beach in California or France, it is composed of shale—small to large rocks. This created many problems, one of them being that the rocks were difficult to traverse. With each step, they gave way. My mother often suffered great discomfort while I swam, as she walked with me, back and forth on the slanted beach, sometimes on a nice path, sometimes on a rocky one, depending on the swim. Also, it hurt too much for me to walk in and out of the water without sandals. Every training workout, slide down the 40° slanted beach into the water. Once I was in, I would throw my sandals back to mom. At the end of the workout, she, in turn, would toss them back to me.

Another problem with the shale beach occurred whenever the sea was very rough. Then the waves crashed onto the rocks, pulling them down the slope. The waves rose abruptly and immediately dropped, ending in a curling undertow, throwing rocks in all directions. It was very difficult to get out of the water during these times. As the waves broke, I would attempt to scurry up the beach out of the water, but with the loose rocks, it was difficult to scramble out before another wave smashed the shore, spewing pebbles in its wake. Many days I returned from workout with bruises made by these stones.

Although the beach was nicer, the tides were just as strong as in France, so the water would disappear twice a day, leaving boats tilted or the levies exposed in low tide! This meant you had to swim at low tide so when you walked out you were dry, and when you walked in, you were closer to high tide.

Folkestone harbor at low tide

Mom's job was very tedious. She walked back and forth, counting my strokes and watching for the unexpected. On several occasions, her warnings kept me from crashing into pieces of driftwood, garbage, fishing lines, boats, and even a hatch cover.

Penny entering ocean in rough, choppy day

Regardless of the weather, she was with me. It was almost always raining or cold, and she rarely complained.

Our daily schedule was as follows:

Up at	6:00 a.m.
Walk to pool	6:15 a.m.-6:40 a.m.
Pool swim	6:45 a.m.-8:45 a.m.
Walk home	9:00 a.m.-9:25 a.m.
Breakfast	9:30 a.m.-9:50 a.m.
Rest/Errands	10 :00 a.m.-11:00 a.m.
	(me—mental training/rest; mom-errands)

Sea swim	11:00 a.m.-2, 3, or 4:00 p.m., sometimes 6:00 p.m.
Rest	Whatever time I finish swimming
Walk to pool	3:30 p.m.-3:55 p.m.
Pool swim	4:00 p.m.-6:00 p.m.
Walk home	6:15 p.m.-6:40 p.m.
Dinner in room	7:00 p.m.-7:30 p.m. (mental training, tapes, cards)
Bed	9:00 p.m.

Whenever I had a short sea training, I swam two pool workouts: one in the morning, one in the afternoon. When I had a long sea workout, I only did one pool practice. This was our schedule six days a week for eight weeks. One day a week I took completely off. I needed it, more mentally than physically. This also gave us an opportunity to tour England. On such days, we visited Brighton, Canterbury, and even walked to Dover via the cliffs.

In my training, I was averaging twenty miles a day in June and a little more than twenty-five miles in July prior to my taper. Whatever free time I had was spent relaxing and reading. Neither of us enjoyed going to restaurants; it took too much time. Instead, we either bought tea and sandwiches from the hotel, or went grocery shopping, then enjoyed a meal in our room. After training and a hot bath, I preferred sitting in bed reading a good book, eating peanut butter and crackers or cheese. It was very relaxing, and I was always tired. We also watched a ton of tennis matches on the television.

Prior to my Channel crossing, I wanted to swim a race. I contacted the British Long Distance Swimming Association (BLDSA) for information. I decided to enter the Torbay 8 Mile swim on July 1. To travel to Torbay, in addition to the cost of the hotel, the swim would run me about one hundred dollars. I thought it would be worth the expenditure because I felt I needed a test prior to the Channel swim. Once I entered, I was told my entry was a day late. It arrived on June 1, the closing date was May 31. I would be able to swim unofficially, however. In the meantime, I had to join the BLDSA. Four days prior to the swim, I was told I would not be allowed to swim, even unofficially. I was upset with the BLDSA and immediately canceled my membership. Later, I received a very nice letter explaining their situation and apologizing for the errors. That was the end of my trial swim, I thought.

Gradually the days drifted into July. Finally, the open air sea pool, a half block from the hotel, was opened. The water was 64°. As it became available to the Channel swimmers, I curtailed my commuting to the Sports Center. That saved me almost two hours a day.

Unheated open water sea pool

Also, with the beginning of July, other Channel swimmers from all over the world started to arrive. Some of these included Sandy Blewitt and Meda MacKenzie of New Zealand, Robbie Phillips of Wales, Tina Bischoff of the USA, Paulo Pinto of Italy. Each swimmer had his ideas about Channel swimming—the diversity was amazing. It was fascinating to meet and discuss methods with other swimmers.

One of the facets of Channel swimming I was astonished with was the success ratio — out of 1100⁺ attempts since Captain Webb's inaugural swim in 1875, only a mere 200 had been successful by 1977. The Channel was a difficult swim. The swimmer's first goal must be to make it; any record was secondary.

Unfortunately, I met a few swimmers who were not prepared either mentally or physically. They had taken it too lightly. Of course, they felt they were prepared. They had no idea of the amount of training and preparation necessary to complete the swim. Many had swum fifteen or even twenty-mile distances, but not under the adverse conditions of the Channel. The biggest was the cold water temperatures. During the summer, water temperatures ranged from 56° to 63° when the swimmers would be attempting crossings. Next, the tides and currents, which if not reached or crossed within an allocated time, would push a swimmer miles off course, adding another three or four hours to the swim, waiting for the tides to get them back on course by altering their direction. In addition, were the obstacles one was confronted with: patches of seaweed, Portuguese man-of-war, garbage, oil slicks, debris, ships, and rough seas.

One young American man I encountered had not acclimatized nor trained enough. For one hundred meters he had speed, but near the end of a mile, he waned. He arrived in England three weeks before his attempt. The water was too cold for him, but instead of staying in longer each day, he curtailed his training. Most of his swimming was done in the open air pool; he could not stand the sea. He never was in the sea for more than an hour; he could not adapt. He knew he could not make it, yet he felt he could not let the people at home down, so he made an attempt anyway. He remained in the water less than ninety minutes. For this, the navigator received $800. The swimmer threw away over $2000.

In the second week of July, the first group of swimmers tackled the channel. Two days prior to the first day of the neap tides, Robbie Phillips and his coach, Alex, arrived from Wales. It was his second attempt at the Channel. The first time, he was within a mile of the

French coast when the tides changed. He either had to wait four hours to get in, or get out. He was taken out. That was in 1975. After three years of preparation, he wanted another chance.

At 4:00 a.m. on Thursday, July 13, Mom and I rose to see Robbie off on a swim. Unfortunately, there was a fog layer. The swim was postponed. That evening we all went out to dinner, knowing Robbie would be going in the next morning. Friday, we were up at 5:00 a.m. Mrs. Scott offered to drive us to Shakespeare Beach in Dover for the start.

**White cliffs of Dover above Shakespeare Beach;
start of swims from England to France**

The conditions were perfect. The sea was flat as glass; the sun was shining. Along with Robbie, Sandy Blewitt, coached by Lynne Cox, and an eleven-year-old boy from South Africa were attempting the crossing also. I was so nervous as I watched each one begin, knowing my chance was next. Gradually, the boat slipped out of sight. Throughout the day, we carefully monitored their swims and wished Robbie success. First Sandy was pulled out, and then the eleven-year-old withdrew. Hours passed. Robbie had two miles, then one mile to go. He was racing the tides. In the end, the tides won. He was being pulled off the coast back into the Channel. After twelve grueling hours, Robbie was pulled out. He could not beat the tides. Only one mile offshore, it would take him four or five more hours to get in. It must have been so frustrating, so depressing.

One of the hardest things for me was to meet his boat when it returned that evening at 11:00 p.m. He had given everything, but he could not beat the conditions. I was speechless, not knowing what to say. I was very happy I had gone because I got to hear all that he had gone through to get to this point. We kept our feelings under control. We just let him share his thoughts and feelings with us. He spoke quietly of how he felt, what he went through. Then he said he would try again.

From that evening on, I knew the Channel was mine. I was ready. Some of the mystery was gone. I had felt its effects through Robbie. I would not let it beat me.

The first tides had passed. Three swimmers up—three down. Over seventy more were scheduled to swim in the summer; eleven on the next set of neap tides; I was one of them.

THE FINISHING TOUCHES

S unday, July 16, I had arranged to swim with my navigator, Mr. Reg Brickell. I wanted him to see how fast I swam. I had been unable to meet with him up to that point because he was on a government cable-laying job in the Channel. He had already dropped some of his swimmers, but not me. He was unsure if he could get back in time to take me on the crossing, but it looked hopeful. I was hanging on a limb, but I did not want to change navigators, because I had been told he was one of the best. Furthermore, I had signed up with him one and a half years in advance. I was at the top of the list; I had first priority. If I had to change to another, I would not have that advantage.

We arrived on Sunday, expecting to swim a little in the harbor. This was not the case, however. Tina Bischoff, world record holder for England to France for two weeks in 1976, was also there with her coach. Mr. Brickell planned to take the two of us out for an hour swim. I was very pleased.

As the boat cleared the harbor, we were instructed to jump in. Politely, I asked if Tina and I should stay together. Her coach looked questioningly at Mr. Brickell, then glanced at me, a smirk on his face. "We better see what happens," he sarcastically responded, as if he felt Tina would leave me behind. I smiled at my mom and she smiled back at me. Just the contrary occurred! I left Tina in my wake. I swam four miles before I was told to climb out. Tina was a mile behind me. Mr. Brickell was very pleased with my swim. He felt I had an excellent shot at the record; he only hoped I could withstand the pace. I knew I could. Before I climbed out of the water I blew out some of my air so I was relaxed. I didn't want to look tired. When I climbed out Tina's coach said, "You are amazing." I thanked him and went to get a towel from my mom. Mom told me, "Great job," and snickered. Reg told me I would retain my first spot!

Besides swimming, I did three types of mental training a day. I listened to a relaxation tape two times a day. I said three positive affirmations two times a day. I put red dots on things everywhere I went for the year to remind me of my goals. I had red dots on my suitcases, my books, and my toothbrush. Plus, a stop sign, red lights, and tail lights would remind me of my goals. My affirmations and goals for the swim were those listed below:

Affirmations:

1. The colder the water the more comfortable I become; the colder the water, the more relaxed I become, and the faster I move through the water.
2. Each time I move my arms, it relaxes those muscles; and the harder and faster I move them, the more they relax, the more comfortable they become and the faster I swim.
3. I am 1000 times more calm, excited, and relaxed because I have just swum the English Channel. From the moment I entered the water, to the moment I came out, I was in the water fifteen minutes.

Goals:

1. Swim the English Channel.
2. Break the overall record.
3. Break eight hours.
4. Swim the English Channel in seven hours.

The next morning Reg confirmed my swim. He had hired another boat to navigate my crossing. I was very relieved, but he told me I would have to limit my people to five as the boat was very small. Besides my people, there would be two observers, the navigator, and one copilot. This did not matter though, I had the best pilot. He believed in me.

I asked Mr. Brickell if it was possible for a swimmer to swim too fast and run into the beginning of the outgoing tide. He laughed and said no. Ironically, I proved him wrong in my crossing.

Later that afternoon, I swam my longest sea training—six hours. It felt fine; I was not cold. In one day, I would begin my nine-day taper. To taper is to drop the mileage each day from eleven days to one day before the swim. It relaxes the muscles and rests the body for the swim. The swim and all of its aspects were falling into place. I was very confident.

Everything was geared as if the swim was to be on Thursday, the 27th of July. That was the first day of the neap tides. The neap tides occur when the difference between high and low tide is the least, and comes twice a month. In order to find out exactly when I would be swimming, I had to call the navigator at 7:00 p.m. the evening before. If I did not swim the next day, I would call back the following evening. This procedure continued until I was given the go-ahead or the tides ran out.

On Wednesday the 19th, my taper began. I cut out my pool training; I only swam in the sea. Gradually, I decreased the miles from eleven to a half mile. By Friday, July 21, I started the protein-carbohydrate diet.

Saturday afternoon Barry arrived from the United States. He had rescheduled his flight so he would be there for my swim. Immediately, he began to question my preparations for the swim. He had spoken with Siga and she had given him a six-page letter discussing the handling of the swim. I never saw it. I had worked out my own training and swim months in advance of this date. The more Barry asked, the more he realized everything was completely organized. It had been worked out since a rainy day in June. Since then, Mom and I had covered every detail, checked, and rechecked it. After we had a long discussion, Barry felt more relaxed. We were in total control.

Also accompanying Mom and Barry on the boat would be Nancy Smith and her parents. Nancy had gone on my double the year before. Her father was a doctor; her mother a nurse. The Smiths were scheduled to arrive on Tuesday.

Mike Whipperfeld, a friend from Germany, also came for the swim, but there was no more room. The only way Mike would be allowed on the boat was if he were made the second observer. Whenever there is a record attempt, there must be two observers on board. All the observers are volunteers; they receive ten pounds for their efforts—not much remuneration for a possibly long day. Some are new to the job; others have done it for years. Mrs. Scott had to find the observers for each crossing. She was enthusiastic when Mike asked, since she was desperately trying to round up enough observers for the attempts. She had to meet with him to go over the rules.

On Monday and Tuesday we bought all the food supplies for the crossing, and I had two meetings with the crew to discuss the details of the swim. By Wednesday, July 26, everything was ready. All we had to do was wait for the final confirmation.

At 6:45 p.m., Mom called the navigator. A force-eight wind and rain in the Channel prevented me from going on Thursday. Everyone relaxed. I was given an extra day of rest. Thursday I spent relaxing in bed, sleeping, and reading. Then, I swam an easy mile and a half. Before I knew it, it was 7:00 p.m. Again, the swim was postponed due to weather conditions in the Channel. I was not pleased. I was getting antsy. I wanted to swim, but I wanted the best possible day. So I waited.

Friday passed as Thursday had, except for one major event. Behind me on Mr. Brickell's list was Meda Mackenzie. She would not be allowed to go until after I did, unless we passed to her. That afternoon while I was out to lunch, Meda's coach asked my mother if Meda could go ahead if I did not swim on Saturday. Mom said yes, if I approved, and if it in no way would hinder my attempt. When I returned, I was very concerned. I would have to decide. I did not want to hinder her, but I did not want to worsen my own chance. Plus, she wanted to go in the other direction. I was not sure if Mr. Brickell would have enough rest in between our swims. We decided to let the navigator decide. He said absolutely not.

As it turned out, her request was pointless. At 7:00 p.m. I was given a 90-percent go-ahead; we only had to confirm it the next morning at 6:50 a.m. This was Saturday, July 29, 1978. Getting into bed that night, I knew only a few hours separated me from a lifetime goal. I was very relaxed and confident. The rest of my group had made sure I would be relaxed; they threw tomatoes and candy at me throughout the day, and told me I had better not get a swelled head. We all discussed the swim again, and they all assured me that I would have no problem breaking the record.

IS THAT THE COAST?

Abruptly the alarm shattered the silence of the morning. It was 6:00 a.m., overcast, and rather cool. We dressed and carried the gear down to breakfast, which came and went within a matter of minutes. Nobody said much. I played with my porridge and only nibbled at my eggs.

Mom rose to leave. She had to call the navigator for the final okay. Minutes later, she returned, very excited. It was on! Before going to the boat, we had to go to immigration. It was essential that we be on board by 7:15 a.m. This gave us twenty-five minutes to carry all of our gear over there and then to the fishing trawler.

Once we reached immigration, nobody was around to open the door. Desperately, we searched for someone to clear us. The minutes were ticking away uncontrollably. The others were beginning to panic. We found somebody downstairs who rang the people upstairs. At last the door opened. We rushed upstairs, only to be rudely told that we had not been ringing the bell for fifteen minutes. There were six officers sitting drinking coffee, and this man had the gall to call us liars. Very slowly, he stamped our passports. Then we dashed out the door. The navigator was upset at our lateness when we arrived at the boat. I felt so helpless. Everyone's nerves were shot. Hopefully, the forty-minute boat ride to Shakespeare Beach in Dover would calm them down.

The *Stewmark* was a very small fishing trawler. Unlike Mr. Brickell's own boat, there was no cabin on deck and below there was only a small stove and a bucket in which to relieve oneself in. As we cleared the harbor, someone mentioned that we had not written down our estimates of time that it would take me to make the swim. We each took a scrap of paper and wrote the time we thought I would do. Even I did it. (As it turned out, my estimate was too fast, as was Mom's. Barry was within five minutes of my actual time.)

Briefly, I spoke with the navigator; then decided it was time to begin the greasing. As there was no cabin, Mom, Mrs. Smith and I took over the rear of the boat and told the man steering the boat, the copilot, not to peek. First Mom put a layer of Vaseline on the areas where my suit rubbed; then she covered my trunk and legs with lanolin. My arms were left uncovered; I did not like anything on them. The lanolin felt so strange, and I looked like a monster. It felt like I had a windbreaker on my legs.

Greasing on way to start of swim

Finally, it was done. I reappeared as we were approaching our destination.

Greasing completed

There were two other boats in front of us, two behind. Four other swimmers were scheduled to swim that day. They were already on the beach. None of them chose to arrive by sea as I had. Instead, they were compacted in a small area attempting to be greased as the press surrounded them. An eleven-year-old English girl was attempting a swim that morning, also. We stopped 200 meters east of the crowd. I did not want to get hung up with either the other swimmers or the press. I had seen it happen the morning of Robbie's swim.

I gazed out at the water a few minutes until Mom told me to get into the dinghy. We kissed; then I climbed into the waiting skiff and was rowed ashore. I stood alone while final preparations were being made for my other observer.

In dinghy on way to beach

"Excuse me, excuse me. Hi, I thought you were asleep. I am a photographer for the Dover paper. May I take a few pictures?"

"Yes, yes. I was remembering the last thirteen years. I have waited thirteen years for the chance to swim the Channel. Nothing and no one will stop me now."

Next, Karl Bennington, 13, and his mother had broken away from the crowd and walked down to see my start. He was a determined young man. He would be swimming the next day, attempting to become the youngest male. (He succeeded in twelve hours.)

At last, Mr. Scott returned with Mr. Taylor, my official observer. Mr. Scott was very enthusiastic. He told me I would do it without any trouble. With Mr. Taylor aboard, the dinghy slid into the water. I looked towards the boat for the signal to begin. Everyone was waving madly, but I could not pick out the faces through my blue goggles. I slipped into the water to adjust my goggles and to check the water temperature. As I stepped clear of the water, Mr. Scott said I could begin whenever I was ready.

Abruptly I turned to begin my swim. It was 8:06 a.m., approximately one hour after high tide. The water was warmer than I had expected. After a few hundred feet, I passed the boat on my left side. The crew was waving and yelling wildly. My arm strokes felt extremely powerful. Everything felt right.

The sea, however, was not as calm as I believed it would be. Waves were hitting me from the left, from the east. On the boat, Mom was constantly moving, attempting to stay even with me. She was really trying to maintain constant eye contact. It was funny to watch, though. She was giving so much, trying to do everything as we had discussed and planned. I smiled at this thought.

After a few minutes, the boat dropped behind, reappearing on my right side. I preferred this arrangement, because ever since my shoulder had gone from bad to worse, I had problems with my neck. The leftward rotation was restricted. Thus, it was more comfortable to turn my head higher to the right side. It did not hurt as much.

At the first stroke count, I was given the thumbs up. This meant my stroke count was over ninety per minute. I just smiled. It did not feel that quick. I knew I was pulling all the way back and had good positioning underwater. I thought, *Oh, well, if it's this easy, I will maintain it.* I had intended to keep my count between eighty-two and eighty-eight strokes per minute. Mom was taking the count every twenty minutes. This way I could keep track of the time, too. Besides, it helped to break the monotony. At the first stroke count, Mr. Taylor told my mom I wouldn't be able to keep up this stroke count. My mom responded, "I'm sorry; you don't know my daughter." He was an experienced observer, and felt that she was wrong. My mom bet him ten pounds that I could maintain the stroke count throughout the swim. He took the challenge.

Unlike past crossings, I was very close to the boat. Never was I more than five feet away. Furthermore, the deck was only four feet above the water surface. At times it felt as if everyone on board was breathing down my neck.

I was given my third stroke count, and then a large Channel ferry came up on our starboard side. It tooted its horn as it passed. I ventured a few peeks. The ship looked enormous from my viewpoint. The decks were crowded with people. They must have thought I was insane, but they were cheering.

Boat rocking from Channel ferry at 45 minutes

The ship created a series of long swells. Watching my support boat dip in these, I wondered if it would tip over. By the puckered faces of the crew, I knew they were not all confident or thoroughly enjoying themselves.

The weather kept alternating between overcast, rain, and wind. There were a few seconds of intermittent sun—a very few. Within the first hour, a breeze came up. At first, I was fighting the current, but it was not very strong. Gradually, its power increased.

Reg gave Mom a small deck chair to sit on. I was pleased, knowing she would be able to relax instead of running up and down the boat. She looked more relaxed. I smiled at her.

That first hour, Barry and Mom were making faces, waving, and smiling. I smiled a lot, also. Sometimes I would wave or stick out my tongue. Usually, I just watched their antics. Once Barry unzipped the fly of his pants and put his arm through as a joke. I returned his gesture by showing him in inch sign, signifying he was small. We had to play little games, otherwise I would concentrate too much on what I was doing and the pain I was going through. I wanted to stay in complete control of my body and mind, but I did not want either to overwhelm me. This was my mom's first crossing, so I wanted to stay in control of the swim for her.

At the beginning, it was very hard to kick my legs freely, as they seemed to be stuck together. Gradually, the lanolin began to rub off and/or coagulate. Little clumps of lanolin were forming mainly on the backs of my knees and my lower back. At first, I thought crabs or fish were nibbling at me. Then I realized what was actually occurring, and was able to move my legs freely.

Frances taking a stroke count

Penny swimming through kelp

By watching the movements on the boat, I knew when a feeding was approaching. I was able to watch them prepare the warm ERG and set up the pole. Finally, Mom gave me the time out signal. It was difficult to reach up and pull the cup out of the hook on the end of the pole. As I struggled with this, Mom quickly told me two hours had gone by. I had swum approximately six and a half miles. My stroke count had consistently been between ninety-one and ninety-three. Everything looked strong. I commented that the ERG was a little too hot, and mentioned how the lanolin felt on my legs. Just as quickly, I tossed the cup, relieved my system while the crew laughed, and began again. The stop was about a minute in length; a little too long.

It was very difficult to control the desire within to talk with the crew; to rest a little longer. Each second was vital; the breaks must be restricted to well under fifteen seconds. Otherwise, the swimmer gets cold, has more difficulty beginning again, and with the turbulent currents, a swimmer can drift anywhere from a quarter mile to a mile and then some. There is no use swimming the same mile twice.

About seven miles off the coast of England, I began to run into garbage. First, tin cans, then plastic bags were floating on the surface. For a moment, the water seemed to change color. At that point, I knew I was swimming through an oil slick. From underwater, it was rather fascinating. A thin layer tends to cover the surface, restricting its movement. Everything appears off-white, like the clouds. The problem was it stank and it was hard to breathe.

Just as I thought I had passed through enough obstacles, I ran into a patch of seaweed. It was unlike any seaweed I had seen before. Through my blue-tinted goggles, it looked yellow; it felt like grass. Concurrently, my warning signals triggered. Usually, whenever there was seaweed, jellyfish were nearby. I had swum no more than ten feet when I spotted my first Portuguese man-of-war. It was at least a foot in diameter; its coloring ranged from white to blue to purple. The tentacles dangled below, being at least two feet in length. This first jellyfish was floating along ten feet beneath the surface. From then on, I saw at least sixty large jellyfish. Fortunately, since the sun was not shining, the larger ones remained below the surface. Only the smaller ones, four to eight inches in diameter, surfaced. By tilting my head forward a fraction, I was able to prevent myself from running into any. A few came very close. On two occasions, I rolled out of the way; another time I had to lift my leg in the air; but I was not stung. For that, I was extremely grateful.

Barry feeding Penny by a pole

Strong stroke and wearing blue glasses

The jellyfish did not slow me down. Two large clumps of seaweed startled me for a bit, but then I relaxed. Some of the crew had poles which they were using to push floating objects such as garbage, wood, and jellyfish out of my way.

As the swim wore on, I seemed to turn more within myself, not acknowledging the crew's smiles and cheers. To counteract this, Mom and the others would periodically give a rousing cheer just as we had practiced. Sometimes my first reaction was anger, *Why are you cheering? I'm going as quickly as I can!* I muttered to myself. Then, I would smile at them, knowing they were just trying to help, to keep me going. It really did help. It was what I had asked for, also. For a few minutes, I would think of Mom, Barry, the others, my family, my friends at home, or Siga. I missed her not being there. Many times I attempted to speed up, to show them I appreciated their support.

I enjoyed being so close to the navigator, also. When he smiled, I saw it; when someone talked to him, I saw it; and ultimately, when problems arose, I saw it firsthand.

My second break was after an hour and a half had passed. I had decided to break at two, three and a half, five, six, and seven hours. I never wanted to reach a stage of complete breakdown, as I had in the past. Because of the colder water, I also felt more breaks were necessary, but the navigator wanted me to limit my breaks because of all the ships in the Channel. He agreed with my compromised plan.

By this break which was at three and a half hours, I had swum ten miles. I still felt strong; my spirits were high. Instead of one glass of ERG, I drank two. A few comments on the jellyfish were passed. After a quick relieving, I was even better. As I prepared to leave, someone asked if I was cold. "No," was my spontaneous response, and off I went.

The last question had caught me completely by surprise. No one was supposed to talk to me except Mom or the navigator. I had also made it clear, I thought, that I did not want to be asked that question. The reason being that once it's been asked, the mind begins to dwell on it. It acted as a suggestion. *Oh, am I cold? How does it feel now? I guess it is cold. Yes, I am.* All this occurred as soon as I was swimming again. Prior to being asked, I had not really even thought about being cold. Luckily, after kicking it around in my mind for a few minutes, I realized the cold did not bother me. I was so acclimatized and in control of my mind, I was able to turn such thoughts off. At that point, I realized how prepared mentally and physically I was for the swim. Nothing could bring me down, or so I thought.

Slowly, my stroke count dropped below ninety; it staggered to eighty-nine. More seaweed, oil slicks, and sailboats passed, besides numerous tankers and cross-channel ferries. The wind picked up; the water got choppier.

Whenever I had a break, a little while later Mom would go to the bathroom. She always smiled as she left the deck, so I knew where she was going. She struggled up to the bow, lifted the hatch cover, and disappeared below the deck. As she made her way to the bow for the second time, I was tempted to say, "Hope everything comes out okay." Instead, I started laughing. Nancy saw me smiling and recorded in the log as follows: "11:52 a.m. She is smiling about something. I don't know what. Oh, probably dingy by now!"

The chop became worse, so I was moved from the port to the starboard side. The boat cut off some of the chop; however, the wind was blowing the fumes of the boat and the copilot's smoke towards me. At first, I thought it would pass, but it didn't. I felt a little nauseated, so I pointed to my nose as I could not remember how I was supposed to relay this to Mom. At first, they were not sure if I wanted goggles or food. Seeing their confusion, I yelled, "Smell!" Immediately the message was relayed to Mr. Brickell, and the boat dropped behind. A few seconds later, it crept up on my right side.

Wind very strong, France in background

Once repositioned, I began thinking about my next break. *It must be close; I'm losing all my power. Nobody seems to be preparing for it, though.* Finally, I asked Mom, "When?" She knew exactly what I meant, checked her watch, and signaled, "Five minutes." Movement on the boat ensued as they prepared for it. Funny, though, I knew within minutes when one and half hours had passed.

While I was drinking, I looked ahead of me and listened to Mom. For the first time, I saw France. I could see the outline of the coast; I was ecstatic. Abruptly, I asked, "Is that the coast?" Everyone burst into laughter. They did not realize it, but until that moment I had not seen it. I had only lifted my head once, and that was to avoid garbage. Of course, what else could it have been? There were seven and half miles to go. I tried to sprint, to increase my pace. It was very difficult, though. I had been sprinting since the start.

The next hour was the toughest of the swim. The pain in my left shoulder had become unbearable. At times, I was crying; it hurt so much. But there was nothing I could do; so I swam faster. I had to keep going. I did not intend to give in to the agony of it all. This, in turn, gave me more strength to push on. I used my shoulder affirmation a few times, and it really helped.

On the boat, Barry was being wild. He tried to take a picture through a porthole on the deck just as swells from a passing steamer hit the bow.

Beautiful Sealink in distance

He was drenched with water, but it did not stop him. Numerous times he hung over the edge, making faces or clapping or screaming. He had a horrendous screech which he was able to sustain for four minutes! It was too much. Finally, I had to ask him to stop. I felt horrible doing it, but it was irritating. Thank goodness, he understood, just as we had discussed during our preparations. From then on, he just yelled in a different manner. It was still very effective.

Six hours passed—the fourth break. As I reached for the cup, I couldn't pull it out of the hook; it was stuck. Quickly, Barry pulled the pole in and fixed it. For the first time, Mom could not tell me the distance. Something was up; this just confirmed my earlier thoughts. I had watched Mike speak with the navigator, then after him, Barry. Then he spoke with mom and Barry again; but as he did, he pointed at something in front of us. Barry tried to cover Mike's actions when he noticed I was watching. From Mike's actions, I knew something was wrong; he made it too obvious. He acted too serious, also. However, he was just trying to do his job.

I was very frustrated as I started swimming again. *What's going on?* No one had said a word. A few minutes later, Mom signaled: "Four and a half miles to go." I was pleased and smiled while I nodded my head. Again, I tried to pick it up, but I was unable to.

About thirty minutes later, Mom gave me our signal which meant sprint all out for two miles. I acknowledged the signal and attempted to do just that. Barry appeared with some type of bull horn and immediately commenced blowing it. Each time I looked at Mom, she repeated the sprint signal. I was trying. As the minutes passed, she kept signaling. I began to get upset. I lifted my head; the coast did not look any closer. Finally, I could not take it any longer. I turned and yelled, "Stop it!" I was doing my best, couldn't she see that?

Little did I know what was going on. Shortly thereafter, I asked for a break. Mom looked annoyed, but signaled, "Ten minutes." In reality, only forty minutes had passed. The navigator did not want me to break; however, Mom knew I needed it. Since I was not responding to her, she felt she had better explain the situation. She also knew I would swim harder if I understood what was happening. Therefore, she insisted on a break; but it had to be a quick one, otherwise I would drift too far. This was what we had planned ahead of time. If we ran into a problem, let me know what was going on.

As I reached for the first cup, I splashed sea water in it. Quickly, I was given another. Mom said, "Two miles to go. You really have to pick it up. You are running out of Cape." The Cape Gris Nez was getting closer. At the time, I did not understand what she meant. I was in mild hypothermia. I could only think, *Two more miles.*

Two miles from finish in France

As it was, there was a tremendous possibility I would miss the Cape altogether. This occurred because I had swum in such a small curve from England to France. Then I encountered the French currents which were very strong. As expected, we were being pushed to the north; but at this time, there were only two miles of Cape left. If I missed the Cape, I would have to swim at least another hour to reach land further north. No other swimmer had been as fast, strong, and lucky enough to swim in such a small curve. The past record holders had greater curves and thus were further south when they were confronted with the French current. Therefore, they were easily pushed northward into the Cape.

After the break, I knew that this was the time when I had to fight the pain. I had to race. From then on, Barry, Mom, and the others yelled nonstop until I reached calm water. Anything was yelled, from, "Come on, Love" to "Viva la France." They were crazy. Barry was hanging over the edge, waving five pound notes, splashing water on himself. Mom kept smiling and giving me okay signals; Mike was banging his fist on the side of the boat like a madman.

Finally, I got the signal for one more mile. Little did I know that this meant one mile of tidal water, then an additional mile of calm water before I would reach the shore. My stroke count was consistent at eighty-nine. It was all I had.

In my mind, I could only think, *I have made it. After all these years, I did it. I have the record. I succeeded for my mom.* I was so happy I was crying. I kept swimming, ecstatically, happily, repeating to myself, *Just try one more.*

Curiosity overcame me, so I raised my head. I saw the shore. Mom was getting into the dinghy along with the two observers. Seconds later, the boat stopped, but I sprinted on. Then a fishing boat approached on the starboard side. It met the dinghy and began pulling it. It took them way off course. Finally, they disappeared behind me. Four or five times I lifted my head to see where I should land. I could see rocks on the beach, and a few people standing around.

Finding landing spot through rocks

I was there. Slowly, I felt the sand beneath me. As I stood up, I lifted my goggles so I could see. I walked up the beach, passed through an opening in the rocks, and looked for the dinghy. Mom waved me on, so I continued up the beach, far beyond any water, until I heard her yell and the boat horn blow.

The people on the beach were collecting shells. They started to back up away from me like I was a monster. I will never forget their scared looks.

Mechanically, I turned and made my way to the dinghy. The sand was so soft I sank into it a half foot with each step. I felt like a drunk walking, not that I had ever been drunk. I made my way over to the boat with only one thought on my mind, *Hug Mom.* As I did, I smiled. It was over.

Penny walking to skiff

Climbed aboard and hugged my mom

I made it—a lifetime dream! My time was seven hours, forty minutes; a new world record by one hour and five minutes. It was one hour sixteen minutes ahead of the fastest woman's time.

I was extremely happy. It had been something I had to do for so long. I also felt relieved. I had accomplished a goal I had begun thirteen years before. It had become Mom's and my dream. Also, Barry had been there; Brian, Carolyn, Dad, Siga, and all my other family and friends were there in spirit.

Reg Brickell called the Scotts and said, "Dean out at 7:40." The Scotts said, "She's fast, and she will be back next year." It wasn't until we were returning that Reg called in about the record. Both were amazed! Mr. Taylor gave my mother a ten pound note, and they both laughed about the bet.

I was wrapped in towels, and a sleeping bag to get warm. My body temperature had dropped to just 95°.

Checked by Dr. Smith

Temperature for a minute; Mom dripping lanolin from raincoat

Penny warming up in sleeping bag

It took us eight hours to putter back to England and another forty-five minutes to clear customs. There were no reporters, no cameras, but it didn't matter. I had reached my goal. I realized I should have left two hours after the high tide but that will be for other swimmers. I was proud of my swim. I received a Rolex watch for the fastest swim of the summer.

It was wonderfully engraved. My daughter, Katrina, will receive it on her 16th birthday. For now, her godfather, Peter Huisveld III, a marathon swimmer and Catalina record holder, wears it as it was too huge for me.

We walked back to the hotel and stayed up for hours talking. We had a post-swim party with the Scott's, all the crew, my family, and the Smiths.

Penny

The Scott's

The Smiths with Penny

By the morning, numerous telegrams had arrived congratulating me on the swim. Those made me feel proud. Everything had worked out!

EPILOGUE

California's Channel swimmer was sent
By the Watson foundation to Kent
She battled the tides
With waves from all sides
And the record was broken, not bent.
(Written by Gary Troyer, my coach and
colleague at Pomona College)

On August 5, still fatigued and sore from the Channel crossing, I represented the USA in the seventeen-mile international marathon championships at Lake Windermere in England. It was my last amateur swim. I was second overall to my teammate Mary Beth Colpo. The USA swimmers finished one-two. Both were Siga's swimmers. For the first time, the USA brought home the team trophy. I was very proud to represent the USA as an athlete.

Windemere six days later

It was a challenging swim, as I had gone on the protein-carbohydrate diet for my Channel swim and given everything I had there. I wasn't able to enter the water for four days before Windermere as I was too cold. I waited for Windermere. Afterwards, on my first break I told Mom and Barry to feed me every half hour and to keep me in second place no matter what. I struggled through the race, but I succeeded at representing the USA.

On August 20, 1978, I swam my first professional race, a ten-miler at Chicago in Lake Michigan. There were seventy swimmers. Surprisingly, the water temperature was 55°. I was third overall; first woman by forty minutes, a new woman's world record. I was nine and a half minutes behind the winner, John Kinsella, the men's world professional swimming champion in 1976, 1977, and 1978.

1ˢᵗ woman at Chicago, three weeks after the Channel

In 1979, I became the women's world professional swimming champion. I trained in the moat at the *Queen Mary* in Long Beach after teaching and coaching at Pomona and Pitzer Colleges all year. I was the "mermaid in the moat."

As for the Channel, I had hoped to return for a double or even a triple crossing one day, but in 1980 I had a much-needed shoulder operation. I was born without an anterior circumflex artery in my left arm and my posterior had been blocked for years. This was the reason for the blue arm and numb fingers. At this time, I can only swim 200 yards every few weeks or sometimes months before the pain and swelling begin again.

Also in 1979, I became the national open water coach for US swimming, and remained it through 1991. I was the first woman to hold the position of national coach. During this time we won Windermere in 1982, the International Catalina Race in 1984, set the Catalina Relay record in 1989. We set the English Channel single and double Relay in 1990, and the Windermere Cup in 1990. Finally, we were first at the world championships in Perth, Australia in 1991. In addition, I ran camps in Colorado Springs for open water swimmers and clinics for coaches who wanted to be an assistant national coach. After Perth, I retired from being the national coach.

**1982 World Cup-Coach Dean; Swimmer
Patterson and Munatones**

1990 English Channel Relay coaches-Dean, York, Cassidy, Darr

1990 English Channel Practice

1991 World Champion Team — Hundeby,
Jahn, Burton, Wilkerson

1991 Pan Pacific Champions

1991 Pan Pacific Coaches

In the ensuing years, I earned an EdD in education, sub field sports management. I also was inducted into the International Swimming Hall of Fame as an Honor Open Water Swimmer.

I coached swimming and water polo for twenty-six years at Pomona College and Pitzer College. We won two water polo Division II Nationals, and in swimming had seven top three finishes in AIAW and NCAA Division III. Between the two, we won twenty-one SCIAC Conference championships in swimming and water polo.

My personal life blossomed as my swimming life evolved. My wife, Claudia Klaver, and I were married in 2003 once it became legal in Massachusetts. We have been together for eighteen years. Much to our delight we adopted, Katrina Lee Dean, from Russia in 2000. She was eleven months old and weighed eleven pounds at the time. Now at the age of fourteen, she has grown considerably, and daily presents us with new challenges. But love is her greatest gift to us.

Penny coaching with Katrina

Frances, Katrina and Penny at Disneyland

Katrina and Penny at Haldeman pool preparing for Halloween

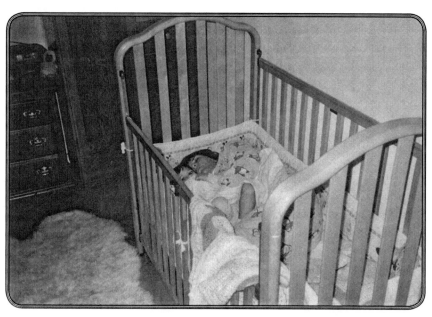

Katrina invaded by Penny in her crib

Claudia, Katrina, and Penny in Alaska 2009

Claudia is an English Professor at Syracuse University and runs marathons. Katrina performs in the local Open Hand in Hand Puppet Theater. I am obsessed with Kansas City Football. I followed Joe Montana from San Francisco. My mother lives in a nursing home five miles from us. It is a beautiful facility. We see her a lot, especially on the weekends.

Recently, I had a total knee replacement after three simple knee surgeries, and after four months, it is still weak. It will take ten more months before I am able to do all I would like, but at least I will be able to swim again.

In 2004, I had to retire at fifty due to fibromyalgia, chronic fatigue, osteoporosis, arthritis, and sleep apnea. All of these health issues greatly reduced my activities. I was depressed for two years after having had to retire from something I loved so much. Fortunately, I was able to share my love for swimming in another way, and began private coaching in 2006, and continued in 2007, and 2009. Now, I am coaching again in 2011.

We stay close to John York and Laurel Lee, Dale and Isabel Petranech, Dave and Margaret Clark and especially Pete Huisveld III, Katrina's godfather. We try to visit each other every year.

In my free time I am updating *The History of the Catalina Channel Swims Since 1927*. I have completed it through 2012, and I have agreed to do four more years!

I hope to never give up coaching completely. It is just too much fun and rewarding, and I can always, "Just Try One More!"

**Penny receiving Rolex watch from Ray Scott
in California in Spring of 1979**

CPSIA information can be obtained at www.ICGtesting.com
Printed in the USA
LVOW13s0712140514

385713LV00001B/66/P